TRAVEL WRITING FOR PROFIT AND PLEASURE

—Discovering a picturesque valley on the Maine/Canada border
—Whale-watching in Maui
—A ramble through America's ghost towns
—Exploring a new resort on Mexico's Baja Peninsula

Perry Garfinkel landed these choice assignments, took the trips for free, and got his articles published in top magazines and newspapers. His travel writing seminar, offered through the Bay Area Writers Project at the University of California at Berkeley, has been sold-out for the past ten years. Now he has put all of his experience, secrets, and insider's know-how into the best reference work on travel writing you can buy. His guide is authoritative, effective, and hard-nosed. He teaches the writer how to propose a story idea, how to get trips paid for by airlines, hotels, tourist boards, restaurants, or magazines, and how to write a polished, professional article that magazine and newspaper editors will want to print. It's a must for writers and travelers who have their passports and pens ready to go!

TRAVEL WRITING FOR PROFIT AND PLEASURE

PERRY GARFINKEL is a professional journalist based in Oakland who has worked on the staff of the *Boston Globe*, *Newark Star-Ledger*, and *New Age Journal*. His travel writing has appeared in *The New York Times*, *Travel & Leisure*, *National Geographic*, and *Diversion*. He is the author of *In a Man's World* (available in a Mentor edition).

TRAVEL WRITING FOR PROFIT AND PLEASURE

Perry Garfinkel

A PLUME BOOK

PLUME
Published by the Penguin Group
Penguin Books USA Inc., 375 Hudson Street, New York, New York 10014,
U.S.A.
Penguin Books Ltd, 27 Wrights Lane, London W8 5TZ, England
Penguin Books Australia Ltd, Ringwood, Victoria, Australia
Penguin Books Canada Ltd, 10 Alcorn Ave., Suite 300, Toronto, Canada M4V
3B2
Penguin Books (N.Z.) Ltd, 182-190 Wairau Road, Auckland 10, New Zealand
Penguin Books Ltd, Registered Offices: Harmondsworth, Middlesex, England

Published by Plume, an imprint of New American Library, a division of
Penguin Books USA Inc.

Ⓟ REGISTERED TRADEMARK—MARCA REGISTRADA

Designed by Leonard Telesca

Library of Congress Cataloging-in-Publication Data

Garfinkel, Perry.
   Travel writing for profit and pleasure / Perry Garfinkel.
      p.   cm.
   Bibliography: p.
   ISBN 0-452-26450-2
   1. Travel—Authorship.   I. Title.
   G151.G37   1989
   808'.06691—dc19   88-19673
                                                              CIP

First Printing, January, 1989

   4   5   6   7   8   9   10   11   12

PRINTED IN THE UNITED STATES OF AMERICA

To my mother,
Lillian E. Garfinkel

ACKNOWLEDGMENTS

I would like to thank:

Annette Doornbos, former program director for Media Alliance in San Francisco, who innocently suggested I teach a course on travel writing.

Gary Luke, NAL editor who made this book his own, and patiently nursed it to completion.

Peter Skolnick, able agent/attorney, formerly of the Sanford Greenburger Associates.

Wes "Scoop" Nisker, for always being there; Daniel Ben-Horin, for the words of wisdom; Ira Kamin, for the music; Dan Popkin-Clurman, for making me computer semiliterate.

Ariana Garfinkel, a better friend no father could have.

And those inspiring writers who have attended my classes. May our roads cross again.

Come, come, whoever you are
Wanderer, worshipper, lover
of leaving—it doesn't matter.
Ours is not a caravan of despair.
Come, even if you have broken your vow
A hundred times.
Come, come again, come.

—Jelal-ud Din Rumi

Contents

TRAVEL WRITING FOR PROFIT AND PLEASURE

Through the Looking Glass Blithely: Welcome to the Travel Writer's Mind-set

That's me on the cover of this book. It could be you. Really.

There I was, newly separated from my wife, alone on the island of Kaui.

"Write," my inner voice kept saying.

"Shut up," my ears heard my mouth say. "Be realistic—you've got to make a living."

Meanwhile, from my hotel room in Poipu Beach, palms lilted in the wind, just like they're supposed to.

At the time I was writing a travel column for *Diversion* magazine, which touts itself as being "for physicians at leisure." The story was about the serendipity of travel—and there I was living it. I played at beaches, took long hikes, read, rode waves for hours, flew in helicopters, and took some time to reevaluate my life and myself.

But life, as they say in Hawaii, "is no day at the beach." They say that on their way to the beach, to the tennis courts, to the docks, to dinner.

Writing is not necessarily a day at the beach either, and the writing wasn't going well on that particular day, so I took a stroll down the beach to a garden restaurant, where I stared at a lush green Hawaiian landscape and consumed massive quantities of Mai Tais. And then I experienced what in other circumstances would have been considered a spiritual epiphany.

That was a good day of travel writing. They get better. They get worse. But either way, what a way to get anywhere in the world that you want to go.

Years after I had been traveling and, almost coincidentally, writing about my journeys, I realized I was participating in a form of journalism known as travel writing. And it was not until several years after I had been teaching nonfiction writing workshops that I realized travel writing could be "taught" (as much as any style of writing can be "taught") as a distinct genre.

Still, I do not necessarily think of myself as a travel writer— or as solely a travel writer—but rather as a person who loves to travel, to meet and mingle with people of both privilege and poverty, to wander among ancient ruins, to meander down cobblestoned streets and along hilltop trails, and to savor pristine moments in faraway places that rejuvenate and inspire a larger sense of self. I suspect you and I are not so different in that regard.

Mine is a work that others would call a lifestyle, as distinguished these days from a life. It is a lifestyle I could otherwise never afford (in either time or money) even if I worked at some high-paying job downtown.

To be sure, we will never get rich as travel writers. But no one lives better from check to check. Picture me or (more to the point) picture yourself now cruising the fjords of Norway . . . now snorkeling the waters of the Red Sea . . . now sampling bed and breakfast inns up and down the California coast . . . now touring Van Gogh's South of France . . . now river rafting Idaho's Salmon River . . .

Frequently we merely cover the expenses of these trips by selling stories and pictures to newspapers or magazines. At times, a well-placed story brings a decent fee, enabling us to make a slight profit. In the best of situations, a magazine will pick up legitimate travel and research expenses—plus pay handsome sums of money for the article.

Then, once you have developed a good track record, with your byline in credible publications, there are even times when government tourism boards and public relations firms representing hotels, airlines, restaurants, and other tourism concerns will collaborate to invite you on an all-expense-paid "press junket" with other travel writers, editors, and photographers, similar to travel agents' "fam trips" (familiarization trips). If you are guaranteed an assignment in writing from a publication deemed important enough to justify it, you may be offered similar free hospitality even if you travel alone—sometimes they'll throw in a car and guide. What these "hosts" expect in return is that much sought commodity called "good press." More later on maintaining journalistic integrity and accepting "freebies." Anyway, none of the above are exactly unsavory possibilities.

This book is an invitation to that lifestyle—and to something more: to a way of enhancing the experience of your travels, whether you plan to write about them or not. Though the book is largely intended for both the aspiring freelance and the widely published writer, it will also speak to anyone who wants to soak more experience per moment from his travels.

What I am promoting here is what may be termed "the travel writer's mind-set," a state attainable by paying close attention to the senses of the moment, by watching for nuance, for social detail. It is, at its most devious, free journalistic license, an invitation to be a voyeur, to look inside and behind places, cultures, and relationships, and then to study and analyze them. It is, at best, a suggestion of a way to see, smell, hear—even feel—more. Experiencing the world from the perspective of the travel writer's mind-set separates the tourist from the traveler.

To achieve the travel writer's mind-set you must be equal parts psychologist, anthropologist, sociologist, linguist, marine biologist, geologist, historian, video cameraman, still photographer, tape recorder, spy, and olfactory recorder, to name a few. Also, when you begin to take it seriously and decide to make a small but burgeoning industry of it, you must also become a business manager, accountant, creative department, janitorial staff, public relations department, secretary, transcriber . . . and, oh yes, writer. For starters.

In addition it helps to be in possession of skin that doesn't burn easily.

This book is divided into two parts: first, a close study of various forms of travel writing, and second, an intensive marketing seminar. I present the information in that order, and suggest you read it in that order, because I am the son of a salesman who taught me two things about sales: (1) A good product will sell itself, and (2) ultimately the most important product you are selling is yourself.

Therefore, the first part of this book will concentrate on the basic elements of writing good travel stories. The aspects of marketing—everything from coming up with ideas, to writing proposals, to nurturing long-term professional relationships with editors—will be presented in the second half.

To the outcry, "Oh, no, not another writing workshop!" I reply: Oh, yes, another writing workshop. The task is difficult (and I'll provide corroboration from other pros). No matter what level of writing proficiency you possess, you can always use a refresher course. There is always room for improvement.

My first mission is to help you elevate your level of writing so that you may approach markets that pay well and showcase your work in appropriately professional venues.

"In the beginner's mind there are many possibilities, but in the expert's there are few," the Zen Master Shunryu Suzuki wrote in *Zen Mind, Beginner's Mind*. I suggest you adopt a beginner's mind in regard to the material presented here. Assume you know nothing about writing. Some of my recommendations about how to improve your writing may seem at first like steps backward, but I ask you to suspend judgment of both yourself and myself, and let the pendulum swing to the beginner's side. At the least, writing in a different way will help you examine your own style with a fresh eye and an objective editorial ear.

I draw on close to twenty years as a professional journalist, working as a staff writer or editor for newspapers and magazines, and as a full-time freelance. I learned the slippery ropes of my trade without aid of a mentor or a journalism course. The newsroom, where one sinks or swims by one's wits, was my classroom. A compliment from editor to writer comes almost begrudgingly. Editorial advice comes in a story thrown back at you, or when a mercilessly edited piece vaguely similar to what you wrote appears the next day under your byline. It was in this arena that I learned to write and, just as crucially, to develop a thick skin when it came to exposing my precious little piece of literary immortality to the harsh light of publishing day. I also learned that inside every monstrous editor there lurked a warm and fuzzy being crying for a little recognition.

With all this in mind, for those to whom work is something you do to fill your time between your travels, welcome to the lifestyle you have dreamed about, and to the trip of a lifetime. Welcome to a life of tripping.

Bon voyage. And don't forget to write.

CHAPTER 1

The Beginner's Approach: Here and Now I Am . . .

Yes, there will be the poolside scenes at the fashionable tropical island hotels, with drinks being proffered at your beck and call. Yes, there will be the introductions to important people and privileged access to heretofore private places. Yes, there will be those romantic moments of travel writing—aloft in a helicopter, afloat in a boat, atop a precipice overlooking a lush canyon—when you pinch yourself and say, "I can't believe I'm actually being paid to do this." Such moments—fantasized by millions of would-be travel writers—are entirely attainable.

But, before all of that, first there is the hard work of writing well—that less savory though ultimately most rewarding side of this work. The reward is seeing your work published, read, enjoyed—and paid for. The reward is sharing your experience, re-creating the sense of a place with such verisimilitude that someone else could feel it as well.

First you must become skilled at an admittedly difficult task: writing well. This is the only obstacle that separates the dyed-in-the wool world traveler from the dyed-in-the-wool world travel writer.

We might as well face the first fear first. So let's start writing.

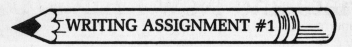

HERE AND NOW I AM . . .

At the top of a page (or, for those chronically lazy writers, at the top of the imaginary page in your mind), write the words "Here and now I am," followed by an ellipsis (. . .). Now, in seven to ten minutes, write as many sentence as you can, each sentence beginning with the words "Here and now I am . . ." The rules are: There are no rules, except to let your mind go free and follow it. Sentences do not have to relate to each other. Anything that comes to mind is permissible. One requirement: Don't stop, don't think about style or syntax. Here's a clue for blocked-heads: When you can't think of anything, draw from your senses—i.e., what do you see, hear, smell, feel? Sentences may be as long or as short as you like. (If you find yourself writing one-word conclusions, however, play with lengths and write long, even run-on sentences.)

Now reread what you have written and look for various patterns in terms of the things you thought and wrote about. What did you observe? Did your point of view change?

You probably found, among other things, that your thoughts shifted almost wildly from the general to the specific, and vice versa. Your mind may have swung like a pendulum from the mundane to the cosmic and back again, from the obvious to the sublime and esoteric, from your outer experience to your inner experience, from looking within yourself to looking outside yourself. From "Here and now I am pushing this pen across the blank page," to "Here and now I am wondering why I am here and now." If you wrote "Here and now I am," period, you are probably too profound for this discussion and may skip ahead to the next chapter.

Not surprisingly, the same general-to-specific and specific-to-general pattern is evident in most forms of writing. It's an important clue to improving your own style, as we will focus on later.

As Paul Fussell notes in his introduction to *The Norton Book of Travel*, "Successful travel writing mediates between two poles: the individual physical things it describes, on the one hand, and the larger theme that it is about, on the other. That is, the particular and the universal."

"Here and now I am . . ." encourages you to draw from your senses, a skill that is one of the travel writer's most important tools. Writing that uses your senses leads to vivid and colorful prose that jumps off the page in three dimensions and four colors, prose that stands out amidst the mass of monotonous manuscripts trying to be sold.

Sharpening the skill of noting your senses will help your writing. Using this exercise, you can heighten this sensual awareness by asking yourself: "Here and now I hear what? Here and now I see what? Smell what? Feel what?" While in the field, record these sensations and refer to them once you are back home at a keyboard—when it will become necessary to bring the there-and-then of Bali back to the here-and-now of Oakland.

"Here and now I am . . ." also reminds you that, simplistic as it may sound, everything you write comes from your mind, sometimes as various unrelated thoughts. Part of mastering the craft of writing involves learning how to "get your thoughts down on paper," as the expression goes, how to record the machinations of your own mind. That entails learning how to follow and to lead your own mind—a pursuit well worth the effort whether you are a serious writer or simply want to understand yourself. Since this is a book about travel writing, I will leave self-analysis to another profession—though there are times when writing forces you to look in the mirror as much as therapy. And it's free.

In its simplest application, "Here and now I am . . ." is one more ice-breaking or free-writing technique that you can add to your repertoire to help get you past the initial inertia that attacks many writers the minute they decide to sit down to write.

Finally, utilizing "Here and now I am . . ." helps you develop perspective—the unique point of view that we read for and you should write for.

Here and Now I Am a Travel Writer

In fact, "Here and now I am . . ." is a key to attaining the enlightened travel writer's mind-set. I often use it as a kind of mantra, chanting it to myself on the streets of wherever it is I am, reminding myself to see, hear, touch, smell, and feel as a travel writer. It is a mental alarm clock that makes you wake up and take notice of everything around you. Standing in a European plaza, for instance, repeating these words, you are forced to observe, to discover and develop perspective.

I cannot emphasize enough the importance of developing these skills of observation; they inform and instruct your perspective, perhaps the most important ingredient of good writing.

And herein lies one of the many Zen ironies of the writing experience. For at the same time that I say the best writing reflects personal perspective, I am also suggesting that the reader doesn't necessarily want to read about you. The reader wants you to re-create a place and tell him or her what it's like there. Readers want to know if the place was good or bad, worth going to, and they want your sense of the place. If anything, they want to feel as though they, not you, are there.

Those people who tell their story in the first person, as opposed to third person, make themselves the subject of their writing. Let me break it to you easily: You're not that important or that interesting. I'm not either. Especially, one would hope, compared to a tiny off-the-beaten-track museum you "discovered" that houses some famous Italian painter's all-but-forgotten earliest sketches and is pleasantly situated next to a cheap and romantic restaurant that serves a tomato sauce to die for.

The writer who buys into his own ego probably loses his reader. In the first place because, sorry again, you're probably not that interesting. In the second because, most editors and writers agree, writing in the first person is more difficult than other writing—because it suffers from sentimentalism, and self-indulgence—and therefore the majority of it is so bad it's not worth reading, especially next to appealing writing that describes people and place with color.

Part of the art of perspective comes from developing that delicate balance between the objective and the subjective, between the observer and the observed. Your job is to sell your point of view without being blatant, without getting in the way. Later we'll get into the techniques of how to do that. For now, think of yourself not as a writer but as a cameraperson on location shooting a film. In the film medium, you choose what to focus on, what angle to shoot from, whether to come in close or pan out. When the film is shown, we in the audience see what the camera saw. We do not see the cameraperson seeing the subject. It's the same with the writer, her medium and her reader. Frequently, when you write in the first person you become the subject, and the reader is forced to see you watching something. The reader gets a secondhand experience through you. The reader would rather see and experience it as though through her own eyes. So get out of the way and *roll 'em*.

An Audience of One or Ten Million

While we're on the subject of the reader in relation to writing, let me interject here my notion about the writing experience. I am thinking of three distinct "experiences," all interrelated. One is the experience you draw from: the gourmet river rafting trip down the Salmon River in Idaho. The second is the actual experience of writing: the process by which you closet yourself away in your garret surrounded by books, brochures, papers, and slides, and stare at a blank page or screen. ("There's nothing to writing," the late *New York Times* sports columnist Red Smith is said to have written. "All you do is sit down at a typewriter and open a vein.")

The third experience frequently gets short shrift. It is the experience of reading the stuff. The astute writer keeps that reader in mind as she writes. To write without thinking about the reading experience is to write in the dark, in a vacuum, with no purpose, to no one.

Keeping the audience in mind is vital to travel writing for two reasons. One is practical. The other relates more to style and voice.

Practically speaking, when writing for newspapers and especially magazines, it's important to have a sense of the publication's readership or demographics—that is, age, income, travel patterns, recreational interests—so that you know what types of information to include, and where to send your reader. For example, you probably wouldn't send a *Travel & Leisure* reader to a youth hostel in a flea-bitten village in Baja California. Neither, I suspect, would you try to convince a reader of *Field and Stream* to visit a health spa in a desert hundreds of miles from good fishing.

Writing with a specific audience in mind also serves as a guide in terms of suggesting how you should write. An educated, upper-income reader of perhaps *Connoisseur* or *The*

New York Times might expect more sophistication in style and tastes. The reader of an auto club magazine, such as a regional AAA magazine or *Ford Times*, might not expect as much.

Imagining too large an audience can be intimidating, even paralyzing. I recall trying to write my first story for *National Geographic*. My "audience" was ten million subscribers, not to mention the millions more who read it (and reread it) while imprisoned in their dentist's waiting room. I suffered a major paralysis of the fingers and total mental block. Stage fright right there in my little old office. Anything I tried to write seemed either too trivial, too pompous, or not true.

What I learned from that—and how I now deal with audience—is to imagine one reader, one person to whom I can relate. I imagine a person who is, not coincidentally, remarkably similar to me. Someone who likes me, who even gets my humor, who appreciates my sense of aesthetics and values, whom I trust and who trusts me. Someone like you. Me talking to you creates a very personal interpersonal tone of voice.

The ultimate test, of course, is in the reading. How does it read? That can only be answered by reading back to yourself what you have written—preferably aloud. If you have difficulty reading it out loud—if the words come out awkwardly, haltingly—chances are that it will read that way silently.

Pretend there is someone else in the room—your audience of one—and read it to that person, being aware of phrasing and expression. When you get "stuck" in your writing, a state that does occur for every writer, go back to the top of the page and read it out loud. Frequently you will find clues in your own words that will tell you where to go, what to elaborate on, what line of thought has been left dangling and needs bringing together.

Beyond Here and Now

So that you are not left dangling at the end of this chapter, here's another assignment that will help you make the bridge from here and now to anywhere anytime.

WRITING ASSIGNMENT #2

POSTCARD FROM PARADISE

Pretend you are at your favorite travel destination in the world, some place you have or have not been. Send a postcard to one of your closest friends and describe the place, how it feels, how you feel, what you see, what you are thinking. Begin the first sentence with the words, "Here and now I am . . ."

CHAPTER 2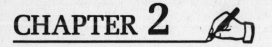

Modeling After the Masters: Following in the Footsteps of Greater and Lesser Travel Writers

So how far back do you want to go? Way back to *History of the Persian Wars*, written by Greek explorer/historian Herodotus (c. 480 B.C.–c. 425 B.C.), who is said to be father to both history and travel writing? That's where Paul Fussell begins in his excellent anthology on travel writing, *The Norton Book of Travel*. I'd settle for the more contemporary Marco Polo (well, at least he's in this millennium), whose *Travels of Marco Polo* may well be the first travel book and is worth rereading if only to remind us of how easy traveling and writing about it are now, relatively speaking.

Polo was the Venetian merchant who with his father and uncle spent twenty-five years traveling the Near and Far East, eventually becoming an important figure in the court of Kublai Khan in remote China. Young Marco was twenty-one when he first arrived in Cathay in the year 1275. His travels make fascinating reading, especially when considered in the dim light of that era. Remember, he was describing a land wholly unknown in Europe. So fantastic were his tales when he returned to Italy that he was nicknamed Marco Polo of the Millions.

Later, while imprisoned after a trade war between Venice and Genoa, Polo drew on the copious notes he kept while traveling and dictated his adventures to a scribe. Though his journal circulated in many forms for years after that, Polo's manuscript was first published in the sixteenth century by an Italian named Rumusio, who is said to have heard the stories from an old Venetian senator who claimed to have heard them from his grandfather. That was the basis of Marsden's classic English version, *Travels of Marco Polo*, first published in 1818 and with which most contemporary readers are familiar.

I admire Polo in particular because he was a natural journalist; he was a precise reporter with a keen eye for facts and minute detail, all of which he included in his book. Such was his preoccupation with preciseness that the book suffers at times from tedium. A sample:

In this island of Zipangu and the others in its vicinity, their idols are fashioned in a variety of shapes, some of them having the heads of oxen, some of swine, of dogs, goats, and many other animals. Some exhibit the appearance of a single head with two faces; others of three heads, one of them in its proper place, and one upon each shoulder. Some have four arms, others ten, and some an hundred, those which have the greatest number being regarded as the most powerful, and therefore entitled to the most particular worship. . . .

He was, as well, a natural geographer, the first European traveler to cross the Asian continent, meticulously charting the succession of countries and other geographic relationships. Because his reports were taken so lightly, however, his valuable contribution to geography were not acknowledged until Vasco da Gama and others charted the region centuries later.

In fact, he was the consummate travel writer, combining anthropology, linguistics, meteorology, oceanography, and most other disciplines, all augmented by natural curiosity and wonder. His ability to charm his way into the inner circle of authority should be noted too. He also kept his reader well in mind, making comparisons to things familiar at home when necessary.

What I also find interesting—and relevant to understanding what makes for good travel writing—is that Polo's writings emerged from the pursuit of something other than "a good travel story." His motivation was elsewhere; basically he was into imports. He was writing about what compelled him, as opposed to being compelled to write. Similarly, those contemporary travel writers who are taken by an experience or a place tend to write about it with more enthusiasm and less self-consciousness than when they write about someplace because they got an assignment to write about it. I can speak from firsthand experience in that regard, having written from both sides and noticed the qualitative difference in my writing. Good writing comes from strong interest, from a passion. That is why I will suggest later that your early travel pieces be written about places you know well and already appreciate, places you'd want to write about even if you didn't write.

More contemporary still, I'd suggest a writer who was recommended to me as the best travel writer of the nineteenth century—Samuel Langhorne Clemens, better known as Mark Twain.

A former printer and riverboat pilot on the Mississippi River, Clemens landed his first newspaper job in Virginia City, Nevada, in 1862. He got his first taste of travel writing in 1866 when the *Sacramento Times* sent him to Hawaii, then known as the Sandwich Islands. The next year he joined a cruise headed for the Holy Land via Europe. His irreverent collection of travel sketches, written as dispatches for San Francisco's *Daily Alta California* and the New York *Tribune*, was published in 1869. The book *Innocents Abroad* made his nom de plume an international household word and made him a wealthy man.

In his preface to *Innocents Abroad*, Twain sets the tone and, incidentally, leaves some good advice for the would-be traveler and would-be travel writer:

> This book is a record of a pleasure trip. If it were a record of a solemn scientific expedition, it would have about it that gravity, that profundity, and that impressive incomprehensibility which are so proper to works of that kind, and withal so attractive. Yet notwithstanding it is only a record of a picnic, it has a purpose, which is to suggest to the reader how *he* would be likely to see Europe and the East if he looked at them with his own eyes instead of the eyes of those who traveled in those countries before him. I make small pretence of showing anyone how he *ought* to look at objects of interest beyond the seas—other books do that, and therefore, even if I were competent to do it, there is no need.
>
> I offer no apologies for any departures from the usual style of travel writing that may be charged against me—for I think I have seen with impartial eyes, and I am sure I have written at least honestly, whether wisely or not.

Modern readers will immediately be struck by his outmoded and overly complicated sentence structure and his archaic vocabulary. Twain both acknowledges and distances himself from whatever the notion of traditional travel writing was at the time, thereby establishing himself as part of the lineage but a step beyond it.

He also stresses that his is but one man's view, and though he says he sees with "impartial eyes," his own perspective is highly subjective—and a riot to read. Such is Twain's irreverence—even toward himself—that he encourages travelers not to take his word for it, but to go see for themselves. Good advice to the wise travel writer: Read all the brochures, read the books (fiction and nonfiction), read the travel guides, read everything you can get your hands on, and then forget them all when you go. Seeing for yourself—as well as hearing, smelling, tasting, experiencing, and feeling—is believing. Spoken like a true native of Missouri.

There are, of course, many others to read in search of travel writing excellence.

Among writers of this century there is Nobel Price-winner John Steinbeck, who in 1960, at the age of sixty, with his "great works" behind him, relaxed and took off on a little travel adventure with his friend Charley, a big French poodle. The result was the very popular *Travels with Charley*, which touched the hearts of many readers. When I read it in junior high school, I appreciated it as a travel adventure about a guy and his dog. Later I understood it on another level, as the journey of life, best expressed in Steinbeck's opening paragraphs:

> Once a journey is designed, equipped, and put in process, a new factor enters and takes over. A trip, a safari, an exploration, is an entity, different from all other journeys. It has personality, temperament, individuality, uniqueness. A journey is a person in itself; no two are alike. And all plans, safeguards, policing, and coercion are fruitless. We find after years of struggle that we do not take a trip; a trip takes us. Tour masters, schedules, reservations, brass-bound and inevitable, dash themselves to wreckage on the personality of the trip. Only when this is recognized can the blow-in-the-glass bum relax and go along with it. Only then do the frustrations fall away. In this a journey is like marriage. The certain way to be wrong is to think you control it. I feel better now, having said this, although only those who have experienced it will understand it.

I picked up an important tip about writing that corroborated what I had already begun to sense as a developing writer. "One of my purposes was to listen," Steinbeck wrote at one point, "to hear speech, accent, speech rhythms, overtones and emphasis. For speech is so much more than words and sentences. I did listen everywhere."

Language is the key to almost any culture. Patois—the special jargon of any group, or the unique words that crop up in some places or among certain people—can capture or caricature more succinctly and colorfully than almost any other writing technique. Listening to people—really listening—and quoting them in their style is one of a writer's great sources for material. And, while it helps develop your "ear" it also may help to inspire your own "voice."

The boundaries of travel writing are quite wide. We tend to think of the articles that appear in the Sunday travel section, or the stories published in in-flight magazines. But once you start thinking about it, much of world literature could arguably be included. Fussell includes entries from fifty-six contributors in *The Norton Book of Travel*, and you get the feeling he is just warming up.

I'd like to take you on a short guided tour of a small sampling of some writers I admire who may not always be categorized in this genre but who each have something of note to offer in the context of this discussion.

The first travel book I ever read—and which fired my wanderlust—was the classic beat generation novel *On the Road*, by the legendary Jack Kerouac. His was the stream-of-consciousness shoot-from-the-hip hip style whose fast-paced forward-pitched tempo bespoke a mood and a music and a mental attitude emerging in the fifties. Truman Capote called Kerouac not the best writer but certainly the fastest typist in the world. Kerouac composed his jazz-in-prose on an endless roll of paper, and it was definitely traveling music. Imagine being an antsy teenager from New Jersey reading:

> It was drizzling and mysterious at the beginning of our journey. I could see that it was all going to be one big saga of the mist. "Whooee!" yelled Dean. "Here we go!" And he hunched over the wheel and gunned her; he was back in his element, everybody could see that. We were all delighted, we all realized we were leaving confusion and nonsense behind and performing our one and noble function of the time, *move*. And we moved! We flashed past the mysterious white signs in the night somewhere in New Jersey that say SOUTH (with an arrow) and WEST (with an arrow) and took the south one. New Orleans!

Besides the hipster, Kerouac was also the reporter. He lists impressions as though copying them from a reporter's notebook, full of seemingly detached images and impressions that together show the whole (from the specific to the general). To wit:

> Tucson is situated in beautiful mesquite riverbed country, overlooked by the snowy Catalina range. The city was one big construction job; the people transient, wild, ambitious, busy, gay; washlines, trailers; bustling downtown streets with banners; altogether very Californian.

Here is Kerouac again, this time describing in *Big Sur* the Big Sur region along California's coast:

> It's as familiar as an old face in an old photograph as tho I'm gone a million years from all that sun shaded brush on rocks and that heartless blue of the sea washing white on yellow sand, those rills of yellow arroyo running down mighty cliff shoulders, those distant blue meadows, that whole pon-

derous groaning upheaval so strange to see after the last several days of just looking at little faces and mouths of people—As tho nature had a Gargantuan leprous face of its own with broad nostrils and huge bags under its eyes and a mouth big enough to swallow five thousand jeepster station-wagons and ten thousands Dave Wains and Cody Pomerays without a sigh of reminiscence or regret . . .

Now, just to show how a different pair of eyes can describe the same place from another perspective, here is novelist Henry Miller, another legend of his time and certainly in his own mind, writing about *his* Big Sur in *Big Sur and the Oranges of Hieronymus Bosch:*

Big Sur has a climate of its own and a character all its own. It is a region where extremes meet, a region where one is always conscious of weather, of space, of grandeur, and of eloquent silence . . . At night one can still hear the coyote howling . . . On a clear, bright day, when the blue of the sea rivals the blue of the sky, one sees the hawk, the eagle, the buzzard soaring above the still, hushed canyons. In summer, when the fogs roll in, one can look down upon a sea of clouds floating listlessly above the ocean; they have the appearance, at times, of huge irridescent soap bubbles, over which, now and then, may be seen a double rainbow.

There are similarities in the images they draw from—both writers are taken by the blue of sea and sky—but there are differences in their styles. Kerouac oozes with boyish enthusiasm while Miller stands back with a more controlled mature eye. The point is that even if Horace Sutton, Joel Sleed, and every other contemporary syndicated travel columnist has written about Waikiki, there's no reason you couldn't do it with a fresh pair of eyes and a new angle. It's what you choose to focus on and how you choose to say it that makes someone see it anew.

In the following excerpt from *Henry Miller on Writing*, Miller describes a moment most writers will recognize, offering his point of view on the writer and seeing.

> If I had been reading the face of the world with the eyes of a writer, I now read it anew with even greater intensity. Nothing was too petty to escape my attention. If I went for a walk—and I was constantly seeking excuses to take a walk, "to explore," as I put it—it was for the deliberate purpose of transforming myself into an enormous eye. Seeing the common, everyday things in this new light I was often transfixed. The moment one gives close attention to anything, even a blade of grass, it becomes a mysterious, awesome, indescribably magnified world in itself. Almost an "unrecognizable" world. The writer waits in ambush for these unique moments. He pounces on his little grain of nothingness like a beast of prey. It is the moment of full awakening, of union and absorption, and it can never be forced.

Though he waxes overly esoteric at the end there—but, hey, it's Henry Miller so we let him—he touches on another one of those Zen ironies of writing. Like the delicate relationship between the observer and the observed in physics, the writer walks a delicate tightrope wavering between being the outside observer of himself and the one who dives into a situation leaving himself outside.

For a complete change of pace and to illustrate how diverse the source of inspiration can be, I recommend readings from *The Narrow Road to the Deep North and Other Travel Sketches* by Basho, the seventeenth-century Japanese diarist and master of haiku, the seventeen-syllable Japanese verse form. A practitioner of Zen Buddhism, Basho stayed at temples and with friends while traveling and keeping notes. He eventually became a recluse, an occupational hazard of traveling Zen poets but not necessarily of traveling writers.

In haiku, a season of travel must be crystallized into a single image. Like this:

> Still alive I am
> At the end of a long dream
> On my journey,
> Fall of an autumn day.

Practice haiku if people say your writing is overwritten. It forces you to condense and distill until you are left with *the* elemental essence of the thing.

Finally, I close this section with an image so poignant that it may bring tears to your eyes:

> Through Mexico by auto: The poverty is staggering. Clusters of sombreros evoke the murals of Orozco. It is over a hundred degrees in the shade. A poor Indian sells me a fried-pork enchilada. It tastes delicious, and I wash it down with some ice water. I feel a slight queasiness in the stomach and then start speaking Dutch. Suddenly a mild abdominal pain causes me to snap over like a book slamming shut. Six months later, I awake in a Mexican hospital completely bald and clutching a Yale pennant. It has been a fearful experience, and I am told that when I was delirious with fever and close to death's door I ordered two suits from Hong Kong.

That bit of humorous travel writing comes from a chapter called "Reminiscences: Places and People," from a book entitled *Side Effects* by a writer named Woody Allen, a man not generally considered in the legions of travel writers but who here demonstrates his natural affinity for it.

But seriously folks—there is a sad paucity of travel humor . . . that is, well-written travel humor. There's a good reason we don't see much good humorous travel writing and it's not because people don't want to read it. It's because humor writing is right up there with first-person writing in level of difficulty. The oddball antics that beset a traveler, the unexpected encounters with colorful characters and other anecdotes from the road would seem to be perfect grist for the mill of a travel writer who likes to add humor. But it ain't so easy to pull it off.

Writing humor is no joke. But try it, because it may be you who laughs last when you get published all over the place. Meanwhile, in preparation, read all of Allen's prose (*Getting Even, Without Feathers, Side Effects,* and his occasional *New Yorker* pieces, not to mention the scripts of his films and plays). Study particularly how he drops in the funny lines at the ends of sentences, setting the reader up in the first half of the sentence with seriousness, like a good straight man, then in the second half dropping the one-liner. Twain, in *The Wit and Wisdom of Mark Twain,* adds these words of wisdom: "The humorous story is told gravely; the teller does his best to conceal the fact that he even dimly suspects that there is anything funny about it."

Reading good travel writing as training for the aspiring travel writer is called modeling. But for those who may not be Mark Twain—or even aspire to be him—these selections may seem lofty models to live up to. Even if you don't think you can write that well, on a subtle level, almost subconsciously, some of the rhythms and phrasings of these writers may become part of your own "inner ear"; they get cycled and recycled in the back of your mind, leaving at least a sense of what works. They may give you ideas for creating your own rhythms and phrasings.

Some writers worry that they will be too influenced by other writers' styles. Some fear that they will be caught "stealing" someone else's style. Not to worry. You are an individual, one of a kind, and you will synthesize all this input in your own manner. What emerges will be in your "voice."

How you use that voice is another matter. Who will be your audience? And what will be your form? Evocative novel set against a Greek island backdrop? Five hundred terse informative words for a newspaper travel section? A colorful magazine piece, travel industry newsletter, or simply a letter home? Perhaps your only audience is yourself—in diary form (of course, prior to his death the wise diarist will have signed a six-figure contract for the posthumous rights to go to his next of kin). All are valid and what you're reading here will improve your writing in all those applications.

The Newsroom As Classroom: Or, How I Learned To Write

My beginnings as a travel writer were less auspicious than Twain's, though I followed a path similar to his. No, I didn't pilot a riverboat on the Mississippi. The day after I graduated from college I got a job, through serendipity and nepotism, as a summer reporter on a big-city daily newspaper in New Jersey. At the time I didn't even know which side of the carbon paper to type on. Until then the only writing class I'd ever taken was what we used to call in college a "gut course" in creative writing. I wrote self-indulgent stream-of-consciousness diarrheic prose, based on a subject I felt fairly familiar with—myself. A wise writing teacher suggested I write about something other that me. He suggested I try to get a job on a newspaper, so I could learn to write about groundhogs, fire hydrants, marathon volleyball games, anything but myself.

What I learned as a reporter and editor forms the foundation of my knowledge of how to put words together. There are other ways to learn, I am sure, but a reporter's job has been the entry-level position for many writers, among them Twain, Hemingway, and a host of others.

That I had been a reporter was probably the advantage I had when I started as a freelance writer five years later. Not just that the credential gave me a little more credibility with editors, or that my byline was published, but that the experience taught me so much about writing, about editors, and about the publishing business in general. Here are some of the things I learned about writing:

• One of the first things I learned was not to use "I," "me" or "my"—no possessive pronouns. This automatically made me write about something other than myself; it made me shift the subject of the sentence away from me. Writing entirely in third person forces you to be the camera, all-observant. And it opens your eyes to the many senses of the world. In addition, I discovered that most beginners' first-person writing suffers from nostalgia, sentimentality, and self-indulgence. It took me years of writing about other things before I would feel remotely comfortable with using first-person, and even in those cases I would not lead with "I" but weave myself in after I had introduced my primary subject.

• You can't editorialize on news pages. That means no adjectives that reflect personal opinion or imply judgment. The good news was that also meant eliminating all those dead words, like "exciting," "interesting," and other cliches. Rather than call something "unique," I learned to show it was unique—and create more descriptive writing in the process. For instance, I recall covering a parade where I saw a woman wearing a hat to end all hats in the category of tastelessness. The laws of libel forbid me from calling it "ugly," so I described the oversized purple hat with foot-long plumage and what looked like stuffed birds ringing the brim. It taught me I could point the camera where I wanted; I could describe what I saw and the result would establish a narrator's point of view without using blatant possessive pronouns and meaningless cliches.

• I learned to economize on words. Newspapers are notorious

for keeping stories short. Editors are always fighting for editorial space; they're forever cutting stories. With limited space, every word becomes important. Using two adjectives in a row is discouraged with thick pencil slashes. In the process, I learned and relearned that less is more. As a headline writer, counting letters in words to make them fit into the allotted columns, always looking for the shortest way to say something, I whittled at words, and studied shades of meaning as well. Headlines became my haiku. All educated me to the precision and preciousness of words.

• I learned to live with deadlines, for all this had to be accomplished in the shortest amount of time, because there was always a paper to put out, and therefore, always a deadline. This is a business infamous for deadlines and ulcers. Obviously, how well you respond to the former can minimize the latter. Many writers actually confess to thriving on deadlines, or at least needing them for motivation to write. If you need motivation, impose stringent deadlines on yourself . . . and then take up meditative arts to counterbalance living with the added stress.

• Writing for newspapers got me into the habit of carrying a notebook around to record thoughts, events, visual descriptions— just as photographers are rarely found without their cameras dangling around the necks. It also enabled me to practice sentences in my head and then write them down before they dissolved into the ethers, as words not written down have a habit of doing.

• I learned how to listen to people, how to draw people out in interviews, a skill I use frequently in "real life." I learned how important people are to stories, and how important it is to quote them. Listening to people—listening to how they talked, how they used language—influenced my writing "voice." I have interviewed literally thousands of people. In some cases I taped, transcribed, and edited these interviews. The way people talk was burned into my mind, and like Steinbeck, "I did listen everywhere." My conversational writing style derives from the effect of listening to people.

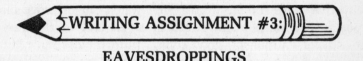

EAVESDROPPINGS

In this exercise, designed to reinforce the importance of listening to people and quoting them the way they talk, I give you license to do what we all do anyway: eavesdrop on conversations heard throughout the day. Carry a little notebook for a day. While on buses or walking down halls, catch a snippet of a conversation that, by virtue of either its content or its characters, attracts your attention. Record whatever you can of the dialogue in play or script form (e.g., SHE: "Write any good books lately?" HE: "Yeah, a little ditty I call *War and Peace*"). Listen for distinctive phrases that tell as much about the characters as a description would tell.

• I learned how to develop a story idea, how to find an angle, how to create a focus. I looked for stories and angles everywhere, in buildings I knew nothing about, in organizations with funny-sounding names, in neighborhood parks with forgotten histories. I began to see the familiar as exotic—to see things with a curious, fresh, almost naive outlook. Later this helped me find travel stories under the noses of so-called locals.

• Writing for newspapers made me aware of facts and figures, numbers, data, and actual information, and it made me question the sources of this information. Attribution, as it's called, is just as important in travel writing. Check sources, double-check times, fees, phone numbers. Be right about your information.

That's the good news about lessons in the newsroom. On the other hand, Hemingway said, "Give journalism five years, then get out." Why? Because the style is limited and limiting. It's based on a traditional formula and structure. There is a pre-scribed voice that all journalism takes, and you can get stuck with that voice for life if you don't watch out or move on. A good writer pushes the edges of style; and in the case of newspaper journalism, good stylists push themselves right off the news pages and into books, screenplays, poetry, whatever. If you continue to write in the newspaper style too long, soon it will be too late to break away.

Among other bits of wisdom uttered by Papa Hemingway was something akin to: Writing is easy, you start with one true statement and the rest will follow. For anyone who has tried, truth does not necessarily come easily. On another occasion, Hemingway was asked where is the best place to write. The man who had written in the most exotic places in the world replied, "In your head."

Well, I beg to differ. In your head doesn't count. Too many writers you meet at cocktail parties are working on great stuff *in their head*, but how much have they gotten down on paper, where it counts? There are good reasons why "getting it down on paper" is not always easy. In the next chapter I'll show some formulas for making it easier.

CHAPTER 3

Writing as Process and Product: Breaking Down the Story, Structure, and Style

If you've been beating yourself up because you have trouble writing, this chapter gives you permission to go easy on yourself. Writing is hard. And if the misery-loves-company therapeutic approach offers an elixir, it may help to know that greater writers have been brought to their knees by the process.

Ernest Hemingway: "We are all apprentices in a craft where no one ever becomes a master."

William Styron: "Writing is a form of self-flagellation."

Tennessee Williams: "Writers age more quickly than athletes."

Pete Hamill: "Writing is the hardest work in the world not involving heavy lifting."

Gustave Flaubert: "Writing is a dog's life, but the only life worth living."

Kingsley Amis: "I find writing very nervous work. I'm always in a dither when starting a novel—that's the worst time. It's like going to the dentist, because you do make an appointment with yourself."

Fran Lebowitz: "Writing is the diametric opposite of having fun. All of life, as far as I'm concerned, is an excuse not to write. I just write when fear overtakes me. It causes paralytic terror. It's really scary just getting to the desk—we're talking now five hours. My mouth gets dry, my heart beats fast. I react psychologically the way other people react when the plane loses an engine."

Had enough? Why go on, you may have cause to ask? What's the payback? For one, the reward of writing well, of toiling nobly—and sometimes with good results—at an admittedly difficult task. Whether a calling or masochism or materialism, we each have our personal motivation to write. And the call of distant places is what motivates the travel writer.

Why is writing so hard? Maybe it's not. It's just that, for most of us, no one taught us *how* to write. And those who did attempt to teach us—our English teachers—themselves weren't taught how to write. They knew what good writing was, they could point it out, they could photocopy it and make us memorize it, but they couldn't teach us how to do it. Sometimes, at best, English teachers might nebulously write "awk" (for awkward) in the margin. It had the effect of leaving the young writer awkward about asking what the teacher meant by "awk." There was nothing concrete about it. Not like in math, where you got it either right or wrong.

When those models of "great writers" were thrown at us, their "profundity," as Twain might say, was so intimidating that it left us thinking of writing as formal, with a capital *W*, something we were incapable of matching. So why try?

Now, though, through the efforts of educators like those at

the Bay Area Writing Project (BAWP)—the program at the University of California at Berkeley's School of Education, which is the model for the California and National Writing Projects—the mystery surrounding the "art" has been codified and understood as a predictable process.

The BAWP program honors teachers' classroom successes and passes them on to other teachers of writing. One of the most consistent themes is that there is indeed a process that is predictable, and there is a structure that is demonstrable.

There is an inherent difficulty to the process of writing. It's called concentrating. Tried it lately? It seems to get harder as we rush faster and faster toward the year 2000; we suffer from information and image overload. *There's too much to think about!* The mind—the ultimate writing device, no matter what software you use—is a wild, uncontrollable beast. Ask it to focus on one thing and it thinks of everything else. You can prove this by sitting down and trying to focus on something simple for starters, like your own breath going in and out, or a flickering candle, or a simple syllable or mantra—or by attempting to concentrate on one train of thought to write about. That frequently is the signal for you to decide to clean the stove for the first time this decade.

To complicate things for the writer, you are asking your mind to think simultaneously in terms of specifics and generalities. You are looking for individual images and moments to illustrate particular points, while trying to keep the Big Picture in mind as well. It's like speed-shifting your mind's eye from telephoto to wide-angle lenses, a procedure that would surely give a photographer a blinding headache. No wonder some writers can manage to hang in there only a couple of hours a day.

Further, you are dealing with intangibles—ideas and thoughts, clouds drifting by. There is nothing concrete to grab onto. Images, thoughts, kinetic connections all collide in the thinnest slice of a moment, and then they are gone again, with no record of their existence.

And then there is the physical reality—keeping your body chained to a seat alone in front of a typewriter or word processor, isolated from social intercourse and other cultural distractions. While asking yourself to recall various sensual experiences, you the writer are involving yourself in a sort of sensory deprivation. This is your work environment. Annie Dillard, the naturalist/spiritualist author of *Pilgrim at Tinker's Creek* and other works, explains best in a piece written for *Esquire* how this effects a writer's precarious state of mind:

> I distrust the forest, or any wilderness, as a place to live. Living in the wilderness, you may well fall asleep on your feet, or go mad. Without the stimulus of other thinkers, you handle your own thoughts on their worn paths in your own skull till you've worn them smooth. The contents of your mind are so familiar you can forget about them. You glide through your days ever calmer; when you talk, you whisper. This is the torpor of deprivation. Soon your famished brain will start to eat you. Here is some excitement at last: you are going crazy. The trick of writing, which drives previously sane people around the bend, is to locate some weird interior spot our brains don't seem well programmed for: the spot that enables you to be wholly alive while wholly alone. A few hours a day of this is quite enough. When it's over, I'm ready for lunch. Lunch with familiar people I've come to care for.

The Stages of Writing

Prewriting and Brainstorming

Too many writers try to write before they've thought about what they're going to write. They play an avoidance game with the act of writing, postponing the event until they have finally backed themselves into their seat. All morning they clean the stove. Finally comes the hour. "Now I'm going to write," they say, and stare panic-stricken at a blank page or screen (the pulsing cursor serving as an insidious and relentless reminder that it has not moved for hours).

Before you write—before you get to the keyboard—think about your subject, talk to people about their thoughts and experiences. Listen to what they say, listen to yourself, listen to *how* things are said. Because our written tradition so directly follows from our spoken tradition, an important part of prewriting should be what might be called "pretalking." Many people admit to not knowing what they really think about something until they are forced to put it into words, whether spoken or written. Find out what you think about this place or person or thing. Then jot down these random thoughts and notes to yourself.

Collect these prewriting writings by "clustering" or "mapping" them on a piece of paper, a practice used successfully by many writers. At the top or in the middle of the page, write a one- or two-word working title for the subject; newspaper editors sometimes call these working titles "slugs" (don't ask me why). Then anywhere around the rest of the page, write other words or subject areas related to the story that come to mind. Now go back and draw lines connecting clusters of ideas that seem to fit together somehow, and number them according to how you'd rank them in importance.

For instance:

> Mazatlán—
> 1. shrimp industry
> 2. local food specialty
> 3. art work
> 4. beaches
> 5. historic fort

These are the things you know about a place that become your outline. After years of doing this, I make a simple and informal outline—but that piece of paper becomes my security blanket and my guidepost. Getting it down on paper—quickly, in a couple of minutes—helps you begin to collect your thoughts and make them more concrete.

Marinating

Now is the time to do what writers were intended to do—sit back and think about it, ruminate, ponder, evaluate, judge, access, remember, reminisce. In short, indulge. Ironically, most writers, in a sort of writing panic-frenzy, cheat themselves of this important marinating stage, and cheat their writing of greater depth and dimension.

Browse through all the literature you've collected. Look up an allusion to a Greek god in the encyclopedia. Review the slides or prints one more time. Play tapes of the native music. Read novels for background. Introspect. Invoke the spirit of the place—conjure it up—and put yourself back there. Marinate in your thoughts and feelings. Fill yourself with these juices of memory. Get thick with it. Free associate. Think about it from all angles. Throughout this process, note the predominant feature or factor or feeling to which your thoughts naturally return. That may be your first lead to a good lead, every writer's lifebuoy.

First Draft

This stage separates the thinkers from the writers. Don't get stuck in the admittedly seductive marinating stage. Stop procrastinating and write.

I find that people generally write in one of two manners, at two speeds: slow and fast. Some write straight through the first draft, no matter how long, driving forward, almost sketching out the story. The word count may appear intimidatingly high but then they go back and cut ruthlessly, cleaning it up. Others work slowly, word by word, phrase by phrase, sentence by sentence, paragraph by paragraph. I write in this latter manner, perhaps because as an editor of others' words I do more self-editing in my head before I commit to paper.

Neither is right; neither is better than the other. If you're not committed to one and are having trouble, try the other.

One tip for those who come to some point in the writing and don't know which way to continue. Some people call this point "blocked," though I tend to see it as spending too much time marinating. Reread what you've written so far. Often the writing itself will suggest a direction. You may have mentioned something that needs elaboration or clarification. There will be a string, a line of thought, that cries to be tied up or strung out further. Go with it, and don't worry about whether it fits there or not. There will be time later to rectify problems of flow and structure. Just keep writing. The trick is to amass a body of work, at which you can whittle later.

First Edit

Now comes one of the hardest parts of writing: rereading what you've just written. Some of it will read so badly that it could cause actual physical pain to certain of your bodily organs. The thing to remember as you withstand this torture is that, as I have found, about 20 percent of what you write is good enough to keep. Editing out the rest is what distinguishes the publishable writer. For psychological solace, I prefer to judge my writing (and congratulate myself) on the 20 percent that's good, not the 80 percent that's bad. One of the sure tracks of self-defeat is to punish yourself for the parts you edit out.

It's at this stage that you can begin to attack your work on the specific level or the general. I look for spelling and punctuation typos as well as structural problems, though I don't notice them simultaneously.

I tend to reread a piece often, first slowly, then quickly, moving from general to specific criticism. I look at blocks of information to analyze the order in which they are presented and to see if any important blocks have been omitted. I scribble in lines or paragraphs where I realize there are gaps in logic that the reader will not understand. I also may circle or scratch out a phrase that doesn't hit my ear right or doesn't exactly express my intended meaning. The truth is this stage can last quite a while for the obsessive perfectionist. But don't get stuck here either. Don't strive for the Perfect Final Draft version yet or you'll never get to the next stage.

Reread out loud. Writing is heard in the mind's ear. And since it descends from the oral tradition, it has to *literally* sound good. If you find it hard to read out loud—if the words come out awkwardly and with difficulty—it will probably be just as hard to read to yourself. For anyone who has heard his or her voice on tape and winced, this practice may have the same effect at first. But bear with it.

Revision

For some writers this is a purely mechanical stage. After scanning your original draft—which, if you have successfully completed the previous step, should now look like an experimental etching by a drunken Picasso, or, as an editor once described mine, "like chicken scratchings"—you realize it is illegible. Retyping—or, in modern times, reprinting—and incorporating all the corrections from the last stage will help you feel as though you are making progress, because this new draft, now your second draft, will read ever so much better . . . one hopes. At least it can be read. You will also find in rereading and retyping that you can sense the flow of the piece from the more removed perspective of the reader. This will help resolve a problem some writers run into after facing their manuscript too long and too closely: the can't see-the-forest-for-the-trees syndrome. Completing this step of the process will produce your second draft.

Second Edit

By now, as a sculptor must also sense at this stage, your manuscript is beginning to take on a life of its own. Ideally, your structural problems have been solved, the holes and gaps have been filled. What may be left are some of those phrases you circled or scratched out earlier but have yet to improve. Deal with them now. Stretch your imagination, challenge your creativity to find words that work better.

At the same time, be almost miserly with words. Cut, cut, cut. As Strunk and White say: "Omit needless words." If there's a way you can turn five words into two or even three words, do so. Shorten it. The more fat you trim from your manuscript, the leaner and faster the prose. Trim down your writing heartlessly. It can even become fun for those who like word games. (Just a couple of minutes ago, rereading a section above, I trimmed "there have been" to "there are." So much for cheap thrills.) In all circumstances less is more.

Also, check for whether you've used the same word too many times or, if you're willing to be really hard on yourself, even twice in the same story. Obviously, I don't mean words like "and" or "but," though I will sometimes change "but" to "however" if I have to keep using it. A variegated vocabulary comes in handy here; short of that a good thesaurus will do.

Which reminds me: Check all spelling. Nothing turns off an editor faster than mispelled words. (Did you catch that misspelling?) Check facts, phone numbers, etc. And check your grammar: Avoid dangling participles like, "Flying over Switzerland the jagged Alps appeared ominous" (the Alps can't fly); dangling infinitives like, "To be well cooked you must boil potatoes one hour" (sounds like cannibalism); dangling elliptical clauses like, "While still a toddler my father gave me swimming lessons" (Dad must have married *very* young); or dangling anythings that modify the wrong noun.

Check to see that you have written in the same tense and that if your subjects are plural, so are your verbs.

Rewrite to Final Draft

Incorporate all of the above in your final draft, the one you will submit. This is the draft to make picture perfect—no typos, or cross-outs anywhere; your name, address, phone, and social security number at the top of the first page; an author's identification line at the end of the story ("Perry Garfinkel is a freelance writer who specializes in . . ."). Manuscripts should be double- or triple-spaced. Some editors don't like you to continue paragraphs to the next page. Others don't like sentences to continue to a next page. Titles are not necessary but are helpful; don't kill yourself trying to come up with some cutesy title if one doesn't come to you. Also number each page. At the end of the manuscript write "-30-" or "End."

Then, to play it safe (read that "professional"), double-check all facts, figures, and numbers. Somebody's vacation depends on your information.

An interesting thing happens in this final stage. The piece *does* take on a life of its own. It flows, it sings, it speaks even to you. And in the final typing you find certain phrases—ones you may have laboriously toiled over to get exactly right—practically rewrite themselves in a manner you had not intended. Go with this new version. It will probably be truer to the style of the piece, because it will be speaking from the true voice of the piece.

A caveat: Another interesting thing can happen here. After eight weeks in the field on a *National Geographic* assignment, plus months of wrestling a wealth of material into a ten-thousand-word manuscript, I had finished and was happy. Happy, that is, until I reread the whole piece one final time before sealing the envelope and mailing it. I read it and decided that it stank. It came nowhere near my original vision. After the ensuing nervous breakdown, I called the photographer who was on the assignment with me and read it to him. He loved it. I was convinced he was lying to save my face. Then I read it to my girlfriend. She loved it. I was convinced she was lying to save our relationship. By the third friend's favorable reading I decided, despite their obviously poor judgment, that it didn't stink, that is was merely bad but not so bad that I couldn't mail it. Unbelievably—to me—the *Geographic* editor liked the piece. His only complaint was that it was too long.

This was a classic case of the forest-for-the-trees syndrome I mentioned earlier. There comes a point in any writing when you have done the best you can do and it is time to let it go. Time to let it sink or swim on its own merits. After too much time you are too biased to determine its success. If you've followed the above stages earnestly, love the product and let it go. If it comes back unloved, *then* have the nervous breakdown.

Structure

To the degree that writing happens in the head and often somewhat nebulously, any anchor that can give formless thought more form is helpful. Both newspaper and magazine styles are based on tried-and-true formulas.

Newspapers: The Famous Pyramid

In the beginning were the four W's. And sometimes five. Who, what, where, and when. And sometimes why. In the traditional newspaper lead sentence, these are answered in the most general terms:

> *A San Francisco man was shot in the Marina District last night.*

This is the tip of the iceberg, the top of the pyramid. It gives the newspaper reader, known to be lazy and short of time, the general sense of the story. She gets the news encapsulated and can move on to other news if she wants. If she wants to know more about a San Francisco shooting she will read on for details.

Each ensuing paragraph will elaborate on one or more of those basic who-what-where-when facts.

> *The man, a 40-year-old freelance travel writer, was found at the corner of Fillmore and Filbert at midnight, mumbling about dangling participles with his last breath.*

So the story moves from the general to the specific. Each paragraph expands on elements from the previous paragraphs. In a manner of speaking, they broaden the base of the story, like building blocks at the bottom of the pyramid. And like building blocks, these newspaper paragraphs often appear to be interchangeable. Without much trouble you can move them up or down in the body of the story.

This is important when it comes to editing the story and a rushed copy editor doesn't have time to edit, or an available column of news space gets cut by half. Then there is no time to edit with finesse. Then you slash madly, blindly, hoping the thing hangs together in print. As a result, the story often reads like a list of facts and quotes strung one after the other.

The "why" gets answered at the end, if at all. Which is a shame. The motivation—the psychological why—is what intrigues me about things. Newspapers, by necessity, often bury this question. I was drawn to magazines because I believed they allowed more room for and demanded more thought to the analytical why of a story, the Big Picture, the What This Story Is Really About.

Magazines: What Goes Around

I envision the magazine style as a circle because it has a beginning, a middle, and an end that may bring you back around to the beginning. It has more of a narrative line; like any good story it has beginning, middle, and end. A dilemma is often presented in the beginning: someone is confronted with some problem. The middle tells the whole story, the nuts and bolts. The end shows how someone changed. There is evolution and there may also be a projection into the future.

The magazine format may be better understood with the help of this catchy phrase:

HEY YOU SEE SO

Hey. As in "*Hey!*" This is the attention-getting catchy lead. The one that makes the reader want to read on. It jolts in its language, in its image, in its challenging idea, in its audacity. It can jolt by sheer rhythm, as in a short staccato-style lead. Bear in mind that you are competing for the attention of someone like yourself, who probably has very little time to read anything that is neither informative nor entertaining.

You. After the lead, you must suggest what relevance this article will have for the reader. *What's this got to do with or for me?* You want the reader to identify, to become involved.

Throw her some statistical data that suggests many people share this concern. Cite a major award that says many other people are interested in this place or thing (people like to jump on successful bandwagons, and that goes for travel destinations as well), or figures that show a trend in the popularity of a place. Rely on the obvious appeal of the subject, such as the allure of warm Caribbean waters to Chicago readers in January.

See. This is the body of the story, the nuts and bolts, the details, the information, arguments, history, techniques, services, etc. Here you can circle back any number of times to weave in more information, picking up unfinished threads.

So. So what? What's the implication? What's it all about, —————? (Fill in the name of your significant other.) Speculate on the future of this place, person, or organization. Where's it going? What does it mean, or what did we learn? End it, for example, with a leading question. In the best of all possible worlds, you can have a key character from the beginning of the story asking the question.

The Building Blocks of Every Story: Leads, Keystone Paragraphs, Transitions, Endings

Leads

The late David Maxey, then managing editor of the now defunct *Geo* magazine, once wrote about leads:

> Magazine writers have a lot of fun in their lives, but there are also small moments of terror and consternation. One is that cold time after the notebook is full, the facts of the story are known, and it is time to write the beginning of the article. It is a matter of faith in our trade that the lead, the first sentence or two, is the place to attract the reader's

attention and, *Deo volente*, hold it for the duration of the article. This is no place to clear one's throat. You're on, kid, and you had better be engaging. Otherwise the reader flips the page, and weeks or months of reporting are lost to the reader. What a pleasure, then, to get a manuscript that bears a lead so shining that the editor knows he or she must smile and leave it alone.

He then cites this lead: "The baroness had no idea that dancing with the handsome young man at the Florentine ball would be an epochal event in the history of wine. She only knew that her husband was furious."

A lead is, quite simply, the beginning of the article. It could be the first sentence, the first paragraph, or, in an extended introduction, the first several paragraphs. In newspapers, the lead is considered the first paragraph, which usually consists of one sentence. I was once told a good news lead should be less than four lines long, about thirty to thirty-five words. The shorter the better.

A lead is like an arrow, pointing the direction the story will travel. It may give clues and drop hints as to where you are taking the reader—but without completely giving away the whole story. It tells, sometimes vaguely, what the context it, but it should compel the reader to read on. It should make you want to know what this story is about. But don't make the reader wait too long or she may become too frustrated to stick around. Deliver the goods early enough.

There are any number, variety, and combination of leads. Here are a couple of types I've named:

The Literary Lead   Open with a line from Keats, or at least an allusion to him. Invoke the literary godheads, or any other superstar it takes to grab attention.

The Quote Lead   Start with someone you've interviewed saying something, preferably something that caricatures the person and helps crystallize a major point you want to make in the story. The success of this depends entirely on the strength and color of the quote. (Some writers are against starting with a quote. They say that's "giving away your lead, and the lead is your limelight." Ralph Waldo Emerson was against quotes on general principle anywhere: "Stay at home in your mind. Don't recite other people's opinions. I hate quotations. Tell me what you know.")

You Are There　This is someone saying *and* doing something. The focus is on a single person and, as in the quote lead, this should be a person pivotal to the place or representative of it. Example: "The tall man with the thinning blond hair stood on a ledge overlooking the Cape Cod landscape. 'This is my palate,' he said, sweeping his arm across the sea-blue horizon."

Time and Place　These generally start like this: "It's 6 A.M. and a flock of gulls is flying low over the village of Menemsha." This can overlap the "You Are There" type of lead, as most of these leads can overlap each other.

General Lead　These are generally drier, flatter. They take the broad view of the situation. They introduce the general topic. "Napa Valley lies some seventy-five miles north of San Francisco." Or "River rafting has become one of America's most popular water adventure activities."

Historical Lead　Again, a general and a historical lead may overlap. "The original settlers of Napa Valley were the Wappo Indians." If you use a historical lead, move quickly to more recent times, which will be more relevant to the reader. Most writing about history tends to be dry and lifeless. Try dramatizing an anecdote from history. Or, if you're feeling really gutsy, add a touch of humor: "Man has been having a love affair with cruises ever since the animal-themed cruise on a ship called the Ark, captained by a guy named Noah."

Keystone Paragraph

So you write a nice evocative lead. You have successfully placed the reader in a serene location contemplating her splendiferous setting. Then someone, darn her, asks, "So what is this story about, anyway? Why am I reading this? What's the point?"

The keystone paragraph, which should appear several paragraphs after the beginning of the piece, should directly answer these questions. It says: Here's what the story's about. Here's why it's being published. I call this the keystone because, like the pivotal stone in an arch, it holds the piece together. The story's *raison d'etre* hinges on this one line or sentence that explains the larger context. Sometimes, the keystone may only be that this is the first, last, only, highest thing of its kind.

For instance, here are three paragraphs from a story I wrote for *Diversion* magazine. It begins with a scenic description, but it's the third paragraph, the keystone, that tells you what this story is about:

From the barren bluff high above Bodie, California, the only sound is that of the early morning wind swooping down the rolling hillsides into the valley. It is a full 20 miles from here to the nearest speck of a town. In this isolated corner of the Sierra Nevada Mountains, seven miles from the Nevada border, a piece of the Old West still survives.

It's not much to look at, just a cluster of empty buildings: wooden and scrap-metal shacks, shanties, stores, bars, banks, and a giant, gray, now-silent mill across the valley. But what memories they inspire: of gunfights, and gold finds, loose women and long winters, the toughest life imaginable—and the excitement of being at the forefront of the hottest gold rush in the young country's history.

This is Bodie, town of many superlatives— the wickedest, wildest and, it is claimed, the best-preserved ghost town in the West. But Bodie today is hardly given over to the ghosts. In fact, last year some 130,000 people came to this remote region to wander among the 100 or so structures and peer into the dusty windows of America's legend-filled past. From all over Europe and the Orient, but especially from this country's own backyards, the curious come to see for themselves how wild the West really was.

Transitions

Transitions are one of the best-kept secrets of writing. They are the glue that holds paragraphs together and, most important, give a story forward flow. I picture them as swinging doors that effortlessly whisk you from one room of information to another, from one subject to the next. They accomplish this smoothly and quietly, without drawing attention to themselves.

They can be as simple as words like "but" or "however." They can compare and contrast. If you've just written about things to do in London by day, you can start the next paragraph, "By night, London . . ." They can allow you to counterpoint information: "Despite these complications . . ." They let you put opposites next to each other. They can get you from one place to another, as in the classic, "Meanwhile, back at the ranch . . ."

I favor the "echo transition" style, in which the last words (or images) of a paragraph are reused literally or as similar facsimiles to begin the next paragraph, creating a sort of echo effect. Here's an example from a story I wrote for *National Geographic*:

> He pointed to a group of figures. "Here's the first lumber camp I worked at, back in 1920. This man turns the grindstone while this man and horse pull the logs."
>
> At today's lumber camps you will see more giant skidders, mammoth harvesters, and merciless mechanical debranchers than horses and grindstones.

Horses and grindstones were bridges or transitions from antiquity to modernity. Here's another:

". . . My children will always be able to work this land." It's hard to imagine anyone working the land harder.

The *Geographic* is particularly adept at quick-turn transitions; because its articles try to cover so much territory in relatively small space, its editors depend on these transitions to quickly slide the reader from one room to another. Here are some quickies that editors slid into my *Geographic* piece (the italicized transitional phrases were added):

. . . The Republic of Madawaska has no political clout but is playing "The Mouse That Roared" to attract attention to itself. *To that end* Edmundston played host last summer to the first annual Foire Brayonne.

. . . When they finally poured the batter, it oozed to eight feet in diameter and they gleefully joined hands and broke into spontaneous song and dance around the implausible ploye [pancake]. *But around here even the largest pancake is humbled by the lowly potato . . .*

". . . In 1965 there were three and a half million farmers in the nation. Now we're less than two and a half. It gets us to wondering whether our boys should go into another business. But what can we do? Nothin'. It's just somethin' we got in our blood."

The river, like the land, is also in the blood. The valley folk sing of their River Saint John . . .

Another type of transition might be called the "abrupt transition." Use it when you have come to the end of a block or section and can't figure out how to get to the next block. Sometimes a complete shift of scenes or subjects is so jolting that the reader gets the point and shifts with you. In film scripts, the direction would read "CUT TO." In fact, film has had such a pervasive influence on writing and on how we process information that readers are prepared for these abrupt shifts. This technique can be aided graphically by the use of a double space or asterisk between the sections, or by starting the section with a capitalized subtitle, also called a subhead.

Endings

There are many different theories about how to end a story. Joel Oppenheimer, who taught writing at the New School of Social Research in New York, once wrote that beginning writers suffer from two things: "beginningitis and endingitis." In other words, they have trouble starting stories, and once started, they have trouble ending them. An evasive writer I know says, "You end it when you've finished telling your story."

To be frank, I admit to having trouble discussing endings, much more writing them. Sorry. I don't plan endings; they plan me. They come to me somewhere in the middle of the writing of the story. They come mysteriously, from the subconscious of the story.

A good ending is almost as precious as a good beginning. Endings create a kind of punctuation to a piece—editors call them bumpers or kickers or punch lines. Often they make the point of the story in a single image. The best endings are accomplished in that frozen moment, in a short scene or apt anecdote. And always in the fewest words.

In that way they are similar to openings—and here is where I can be of some help. I often find an ending by reinvoking or re-creating an image from the beginning of the piece. Now your piece *will* naturally come full circle.

To end a story with a forward pitch, ask your readers a leading question. Make them project or at least speculate into the future. This keeps the story alive in their minds well after they've put down your piece. All the better.

There is a great danger in writing cliche-ridden endings—especially in the travel genre. If you wrote anything like "As the sun sets on the tiny fishing island . . ." before you read this book, I forgive you for you knew not what you were doing. Also, let go of: "And that's the Bay of Napolo, land of many . . ." I know that's the Bay of Napolo! Didn't I just read the tedious copy?

MADAWASKA DOWN EAST WITH A FRENCH ACCENT

By Perry Garfinkel

HEY: an attention-getting lead →

Gedeon Corriveau lives on the edge—on the edge of two countries, the edge of two cultures, the edge of past and future. From this century-old mill in Upper Frenchville, Maine, where he runs

Superlative →

one of the last buckwheat-grinding operations in the valley, he looked down his long treelined driveway at U.S. Route 1 as it nears the end of its 2,360-mile odyssey from Key West, Florida. Just across the road is the Saint John River and just across the river is the town of St. Hilaire in New Brunswick, Canada.

Keystone paragraph ("this is a story about . . .") →

Defines geographic location →

This is the upper Saint John River Valley, also known as Madawaska. This remote region, where the northernmost stretch of Maine meets the westernmost stretch of New Brunswick, lies some 200 miles from either Bangor or Quebec City (map, pages 386-7). It is isolated by the green womblike mountains, the whims of international boundaries, and the quirks of cultural history.

YOU: reader identifies with people →

The 60,000 people who live along the hundred miles from Grand Falls, New Brunswick, to Allagash, Maine, think of themselves not so much as Canadians or Americans, but as citizens of a country in between. When I asked 19-year-old Patsy Bernier of Fort Kent, Maine, which country she was from, she stated: "The valley is my country."

Why this place→
is unique
    Life at this border has its idiosyncrasies. A baby born to an American family living in the town of Madawaska, Maine, will most likely enter the world in Edmundston, New Brunswick—since Madawaska has no hospital—and therefore can claim dual citizenship according to both United States and Canadian law. Intermarriage between the valley's Canadians and Americans is so common you need a scorecard to keep track. Money games are even trickier, with exchange rates for Canadian and American dollars fluctuating with the fickleness of the weather.

Transitional→
phrase
    Despite these complications, the three border crossings along the upper Saint John River—at van Buren, Madawaska, and Fort Kent—are among
Superlative→ the busiest along the entire length of the United States—Canada boundary. This may be due, at
Major theme→ least in part, to the fact that the blood of family ties runs thicker here than do the international waters of the Saint John.

Picks up lead→
    And, as much as anyone's, the story of the Corriveau family is the story of the valley.

    Gedeon Corriveau, born in Upper Frenchville, is a loader for Fraser Paper, Limited, where he has worked 25 of his 53 years. In the valley, if a man
Major industries→ isn't growing potatoes, he's likely working for the paper industry. Between the Canadian pulp mill and the U. S. paper mill, Fraser puts something on the table of almost every family.

    Gedeon's wife, Aline, was born in St. Hilaire on the other side of the Saint John—"across." She teaches French to second and third graders. Several generations back, both their families emigrated from France to Quebec and then made their way to the valley. They are devout Catholics and attend church regularly, where the mass is celebrated in French.

"This's gonna be the last year I grind buckwheat," Gedeon told me in a singsongy patois that
managed to combine Maine drawl, Canadian twang,
and French twist. He wiped his lean, weather-
worn face and dumped a barrelful of grain into the
antique grinder. "No matter how I figure it, I will
come out in the red." His eight-year-old daughter
Nicole, a blue-eyed blonde, and dark-haired Su-
san Thibault, one of Nicole's 42 cousins from across,
played on the steps of the mill where buckwheat
sprouts peeked through the cracks.

"Buckwheat used to be a major crop in these
parts. We used it for everything. The walls of my
house are insulated with it. I still heat with buckwheat hulls. But at this point grinding buckwheat
is more like a community service for me. Everyone in the valley who makes *ployes* buys their
buckwheat from me." Ployes are buckwheat pancakes, and everyone in the valley eats them.

In the kitchen Aline poured buckwheat batter
on the top of the wood-burning stove. Four handsome blond Corriveau girls bustled and giggled
their way around, preparing mashed potatoes, fiddleheads, brisket, and bread, singing a French
song.

Mother Tongue Once Forbidden

Over dinner the conversation was politely in
English. If I had not been there, they would be
speaking the local French, a combination of Canadian French and an archaic idiom traced to the
17th-century France and laced with the nautical
terminology of those French ancestors who origi-
nally settled and farmed a land that they called
l'Acadie—Acadia—along the shores of the bay of
Fundy and its inlets. A majority of the people in
the upper Saint John Valley speak this dialect as

their mother tongue, but until ten years ago Maine forbade children to speak it in school. Then, in 1970, valley educators designed a bilingual education program with a grant under the Elementary and Secondary Education Act, and it became a model program throughout the U.S.

**Transition from→
general to
specific**

I got a look at the bilingual program when I accompanied Nicole to her second-grade French class at the Dr. Levesque School in Upper Frenchville. The teacher, Claudette Paradis Violette, told me before the class started, "The parents who were denied the right to speak French are delighted their children can speak bilingually now." She knew because she was one of those parents. "Most of these children's great-great-grandfathers were Acadians. But at this age they don't yet grasp the concept of ancestry—though it's never too soon to try."

She opened the lesson with some Acadian history—in French. Turning to the group of young faces, she asked, "*Qui étaient ces Acadiens?* Who were these Acadians?"

**Dialogue in→
dramatic narrative
form**

"Indians?" tried one youngster.

Nicole raised her hand, pushing it higher, bubbling with enthusiasm. "They were people who came from France," she answered, ironically in English. She was right, of course. French colonists came in the 17th century to what is now coastal Nova Scotia and the Bay of Fundy. They brought their own dialect from the province of Poitou, south of the Loire River—along with their own customs, food, and dress, plus an independent spirit and the farmer's stubborn streak. Alternately controlled by the French and the English, they were finally ordered to take an oath of allegiance in 1755 to George II of England. When they refused, Governor Charles Lawrence of Nova Scotia called all men and boys to the St. Charles

**Transition to→
history**

Church in Grand Pré and ordered the eviction of all Acadians—*"le grand dérangement."* At gunpoint they were herded onto ships and scattered from Quebec to Louisiana.

Over the years small groups made their way back to resettle along the Saint John River. In June of 1785, a band of perhaps ten families came ashore at St. David on the southern banks, and soon had settled both sides. The names of those first settlers—Duperre, Daigle, Cyr, Fournier— echo today throughout the Madawaska region.

Transition to now→ Local interest in Acadian history is growing as fast as fiddleheads. In 1979 Madawaska, Maine, celebrated its second annual Acadian Festival Week, simultaneously commemorating June 28— declared Acadian Day by the state of Maine in 1978—and the 375th anniversary of the landing of the Acadians in North America. . . .

Living Between Two Worlds

Transition using→
quote
"We were forgotten territory," said Oneil Clavet of Edmundston, who is doing everything he can to help people remember it. "I would say it has to do with the fact that Madawaskans had to live so long without knowing whether they belonged to the United States or Canada. Look here," he said,

History→ pushing a map at me. "For 59 years this area was a bone of border contention because of vagueness in the 1783 Treaty of Versailles. Not until the Webster-Ashburton Treaty of 1842 could the people of the valley claim a country. But by declaring seventy miles of the Saint John River the border, that treaty effectively made an international community of the valley, and in many instances divided families into two nationalities.

"I prefer to call myself a citizen of La République du Madawaska," Oneil earnestly declared. He was referring to the original name for the territory, borrowed from the Malecite word meaning "land of the porcupines," an apt image for the some-times prickly valley characters. Now Oneil un-furled a flag of the republic, then pulled out a draft of the republic's constitution.

Wait a second! Is this a real republic? In North America? Or am I cornered with the leader of an international conspiracy?

But before my mind could run wild, Oneil was quick to remind me the republic is a myth. The Republic of Madawaska has no political clout but is playing *The Mouse That Roared* to attract atten-tion to itself.

Transition→ To that end Edmundston played host last sum-mer to the first annual Foire Brayonne. (A bray, a tool regional farmers used for breaking flax, has become a modern-day symbol for Madawaskans.) If there was not a Mardi Gras of the north before, there is now. The downtown streets were blocked off and jammed for a week with 70,000 people. Their high-spirited French blood ran hot as they celebrated their ancestry in cuisine, dance, dress, parades, and competitions.

The highlight of the occasion was the attempt by Jeannine Albert and Alberic Pelletier and their families and friends to make the world's largest ploye, with bulky and uncooperative pans, poles, paddles, forklifts, and tractors. When they finally poured the batter, it oozed to eight feet in diame-ter and they gleefully joined hands and broke into spontaneous song and dance around the implausi-ble ploye.

Transition to→
potatoes But around here even the largest pancake is humbled by the lowly potato, as this local "Potato Song" laments:

Use of folklore→

> *I am a farmer on the Saint John River.*
> *I plant potatoes to pay the income tax.*
> *The collectors have arrived and they are*
> *encamped at St. Agatha.*
> *They've come to take what little money*
> *we've lately saved.*

"Baked, mashed, or French fries?" the waitress asked, as all waitresses in the valley automatically inquire.

"No potatoes today, thanks," I deferred, still remembering an overindulgence in oversize ployes. By the look on her face I knew I had committed the ultimate insult here in potato country.

Superlative→
The valley is, and has been for a long time, one of the largest potato-producing regions in the United States. The American side is part of Maine's Aroostook County, which accounts for 90 percent of the state's harvested acreage. In potato production Maine ranks just behind Idaho and Washington.

Visual→
description
From the air the valley appears as a patchwork of brown corduroy overalls, held up by long green suspenders leading to the Saint John River— remnants of a centuries-old method of farming which gave every farmer access to the river water. Part of the reason potatoes grow so well here is the valley's natural drainage system plus a good ratio of clay, sand, and organic components. . . .

A Temptation and a Proposal

SO: transition→
leading to ending
Months after leaving the valley—back in my urban environment where I sometimes wonder whether all the amenities are worth the price, where it sometimes seems unnatural to be living 250 miles from my parents, where I sometimes feel anonymous in the city's sea of humanity—I find myself valuing the virtues of these valley

people more and more. I am often tempted to trade urban slick for country hick and a warming evening singing old songs with old friends.

Recall earlier → image   But of all my valley memories, it is the face of eight-year-old Nicole Corriveau that keeps coming back to me, circled in gold, angelically pure. Bright eyed, naive, but learning fast, Nicole *is* the upper Saint John River Valley. Child of a mélange of cultures, a child of our times—the valley's most valuable natural resource.

Kicker-style → ending   "If I come back in 15 years, will you marry me?" I asked her one day. She smiled coyly but did not answer, later giggling over my proposal with her cousin. It was I who was being naive. In 15 years Nicole would change—as the valley would change. But one could hope.

□

Style, Personal and Otherwise

Before developing a personal style or voice, there are some basics of style to which all writers should adhere. From these fundamentals your own voice will emerge.

Subject/Verb/Object

You probably learned this all in about fifth grade and, like the rest of us, forgot it by sixth grade. Simply stated, a sentence begins with the subject, is followed immediately by a verb, and then by an object. Someone/does/something. Following this structure produces simple, uncomplicated, understandable sentences that are slanted forward and move quickly. Too many writers obfuscate their message by using complicating sentence structures—that is, compound, complex sentences with many clauses, parentheses, and other grammatical fleur-de-lis.

People write this way when they are trying to impress you with how well they write—a common mistake of insecure writers. We lean on complex structure to demonstrate our ability with words, often leaving things dangling for our effort. We write this way because a long time ago someone told us that's how Real Writers write.

Complex writing forces the reader to fight for information, struggling through convoluted sentences. It gets in the way of what you have to say.

Most business writing also suffers from too much complexity. Douglas Mueller of the Gunning-Mueller Clear Writing Institute, based in Santa Barbara, California, once calculated that businesses lose millions of dollars a year due to "foggy," confusing communiqués. The Institute makes a lot of money each year telling captains of industry what they could read for free in Strunk and White's *Elements of Style*: Omit needless words. Don't overwrite. The Clear Writing Fog Index breaks down a sampling of one hundred words to determine at what grade level you write. Most score at about eighth grade.

Hemingway's highly imitated style drew its strength from terse, staccato, fast-paced prose that resulted from writing simply. This, in turn, probably resulted from his earliest writing as a newspaper journalist. Though the following section from *A Farewell To Arms* contains sentences that are not all simple, in the strictest grammatical sense, they start with subjects and move quickly to verbs:

> The major asked me to have a drink with him and two other officers. We drank rum and it was very friendly. Outside it was getting dark. I asked what time the attack was to be and they said as soon as it was dark. I went back to the drivers. They were sitting in the dugout talking and when I

came in they stopped. I gave them each a package of ciga-
rettes. . . . Manera lit his lighter and passed it around. The
lighter was shaped like a Fiat radiator. I told them what I
had learned.

Someone/does/something. Hemingway was the master at it.

I am not suggesting you write only simple sentences. That
would be boring. But I am suggesting you take a beginner's
mind. Write more simply, and you will write better.

Stay in Active Voice, Not Passive

Flashback. It's Miss Goodyear's ninth-grade English class.
Quick review. Active: "John put the chalk down." Passive:
"The chalk was put down by John." In the first, your attention
is focused on John. In the second, you're focused on the chalk.
You can control the reader's object of attention. Putting the
subject at the beginning of the sentence practically forces you
to write in the active voice. Active voice is just that—action—
whereas passive voice back-peddles. You want your reader
moving forward with an activated mind.

Omit Needless Words

I can sum up seventy-eight pages by the aforementioned
gurus of grammar, Strunk and White, in nine words: "Omit
needless words, omit needless words, omit needless words."
And I just saw six more I could cut.

If you can make a simple cut from "the dog that was lost" to
"the lost dog," you will streamline your product and keep your
prose clean. What you're doing is polishing, polishing, polishing. Trimming, trimming, trimming. Making a setting for those
gems of brilliance.

And then, there's all that deadwood verbiage we inherited

from law journals or places where the walls are dark-panelled. "At the present time" (now). "In the party of" (with). "In the near future" (soon).

Murder Your Darlings

Maria Shaw, currently managing editor of *Travel & Leisure* magazine, once told me her favorite piece of advice for writers: "Murder your darlings!"

She was referring to those little phrases you've written that make you feel like a legend in your own mind, that reveal the budding genius of your talent. On such thin evidence we then construct major sections around this phrase—only to discover later the phrase was less than brilliant. A general rule of thumb: Any phrase that's cuter than Shirley Temple should probably get axed. (*Like that one?*) Recognizing these darlings is not easy, but a sure sign is that if you feel the need for a second opinion, you might already have spotted the bugger.

Avoid Cliches Like a Bad Plague

Cliches are crutches, phrases writers use when they aren't willing to sit there a couple of more minutes—or a couple of more hours—and concoct a new way of phrasing something. Cliches are the direct result of lazy writing.

Travel writing particularly is prone to cliches. Look, how many other adjectives can you think of to describe a fishing village after "quaint"? And have you ever seen a Northern California redwood tree that *wasn't* "majestic"?

Avoiding a cliche may be as simple as restructuring the sentence so that you are not left wracking your brains for another adjective. Create metaphors, similes, or comparisons. Instead of saying, "The street was lined with majestic redwoods," try: "The redwoods lined the street like tall silent soldiers." Give the tree action ("redwoods lined . . ."). Or, as in the next suggestion, show the tree.

Show, Don't Tell

"Majestic" tells us it's majestic. It doesn't show us it's majestic. Words like "exciting," "interesting," "beautiful" all *tell*; they don't *show*.

The best way I know to get around cliches is to show—perferably in colors, in sizes, in numbers, in lengths—with facts and details. For example: "The redwoods rose from the forest floor to a height of more than 300 feet."

Rather than telling us, "It was an exciting river trip," show us: "The canoe hit a boulder and flipped over. I flew from the vessel, landed on my backside, and slid into the rushing white rapids." Pick a detail from the "wonderful dinner," as in, "The pears flambé were served while the Boston Pops played *The 1812 Overture* in the background."

"Show, don't tell" means the writer must draw from her visual recollections, as well as her other sensory experiences. Keep chanting "Here and now I am" as you search for ways to elude cliches.

Write to the Beat of a Different Drummer

I have been playing drums since I was in second grade. "What does that have to do with writing?" you may ask. Nothing, or so I too thought. I always thought of writing and drumming as two very different forms of self-expression, one cerebral, the other more visceral. Then I realized how often writing is referred to in rhythmic terms: We speak of a "cadence," we talk about "beats" and "phrasing," we allude to "timing" and "pacing." One writes in a "staccato" style or "flowingly" and "fluidly."

I am not proposing you go buy a conga drum, though it's a great release after a day at a desk. But I am suggesting a sensitivity to the rhythm of your writing. Listen for it; listen to it.

Tell the Story

At the heart of every good travel story is just that—a good story. Told through the stylistic use of anecdotes, a good travel piece makes you feel as though you're there. Ms. Shaw, the *Travel & Leisure* editor, once suggested that the best travel writers are novelists because they have such a strong sense of story—of people and of place and of a certain dynamic tension between the two. Novelists also have a keen eye for social detail, for the minutiae of a moment. Look for those moments, pounce on them as Henry Miller might, and re-create them in your travel stories in the form of anecdotes. Being able to reflect a destination or a travel experience through exemplary and engaging stories will also help you when you approach an editor with an idea, either in writing or in person. Following is a piece I wrote for *Travel & Leisure* utilizing an anecdote to get into a story about whale-watching cruises in Hawaii.

Whale-Watching in Maui

It's love at first sight

by Perry Garfinkel

In downtown Lahaina on the island of Maui an anonymous adage on a T-shirt reads: "Of all God's creatures large and small, the whale is the most wondrous of them all." This sentiment begins to make sense the moment the captain kills the engines of the boat. We are silently afloat on a 61-foot yacht in deep Pacific waters surrounded by the turquoise-touched islands of Maui, Lanai, Molokai and Kahoolawe. Below us we can feel—like islands themselves—the whales.

This is the Auau Channel, winter breeding ground for an estimated 500 humpback whales. We are privileged spectators of a rare natural phenomenon, in waters protected by the National Marine Fisheries Service.

Nothing we have heard or read, however, has prepared us adequately for this moment, electric with excitement. We have become aware that somewhere beneath the surface there is an awesome presence whose intensity seems to transcend the fact that it weighs about 40 tons—a fact unfathomable to this 160-pound Homo sapiens, anyway. We feel an eerie sense of connection and communication with these mammals of the deep. Recent research by marine mammal biologists Roger Payne and John Lilly, among others, confirms that cetaceans communicate by a system of "songs" and navigate by sonar more sophisticated than anyone ever thought.

"Thar she blows!" shouts a tanned man in a red Jantzen from the starboard side of the boat. All eyes and telephoto lenses turn. From not more than 75 yards off we hear a ferocious roar, the sound of air escaping the whale's lungs at 300 mph. Then, almost in front of us, the whale surfaces, its black back glistening in the sun. We scurry to the bow for a better look. In slow motion, the whale flicks its flukes and dives. Then silence. We and the whale are locked in a battle of wits.

Then, with all its surging power, the great behemoth breaches alongside the boat. The air ripples. We are stunned by its immensity and struck by the realization that the whale's jumping gesture is a kind of message to us—if nothing more than a flashy way of acknowledging our presence and asserting its own. In that moment we begin to understand why whales are associated with things mythic and mystic.

Whales have been a part of Hawaii's lore almost from the beginning. By the 1840s, the tenacious whalers from New England had discovered the bounty in these warm Hawaiian waters. Up to 500 vessels could be found docked in the harbor at Lahaina from December to May, when the whales mate and calve. Much to the chagrin of the missionaries, Lahaina became known as a popular watering hole for weary sailors.

Things have not changed much in more than a century. Lahaina is still considered Maui's busiest night spot, and whales remain a focal point—though now they're watched, not slaughtered. The sheltered waters between Maui and Lanai are one of the few places in the world where a whale nursery can be observed at such close range. Scientists have known this a long time and taken pains not to disturb the whales. But in the 1970s, publicity brought increasing numbers of whale enthusiasts, and their overzealousness became such a problem that heavy fines were established for violators of whale harassment laws. Spectators must now stay at least 300 yards from them in the breeding and calving grounds.

Many people feel that the recent renaissance of interest in whales may not have come about soon enough. "There's one good reason to see the whales now—they may not be around later," says Donald White, president of Greenpeace Hawaii, which sponsors save-the-whale campaigns. Humpbacks, the official Hawaiian marine mammal, were placed on the endangered species list in 1970. Maybe 1,000 are left in the North Pacific waters—about seven percent of the original population.

A whale-watching cruise is the best way to learn about the mystery and majesty of these gentle sea creatures and the important efforts being made to protect them. That's how Dan McSweeney and Rick Chandler feel. The pair run Tale of the Whale, the only whale-watching operation off the Big Island of Hawaii, where the humpbacks also congregate. Their 28-foot trimaran, equipped with earphones and a video show of the sounds and underwater sights of whales, scouts the central coast. Cruises of 1½ to three hours depart from Keauhou Bay; fares are about $15 for adults, $10 children.

Back on Maui, even before you step on board a vessel, you can raise your whale consciousness by strolling through Whaler's Village. There's a fascinating collection of artifacts, records and scrimshaw elegantly showcased around the Kaanapali Beach mall. Several nonprofit organizations are dedicated to enlightening the public about whales and dolphins and sponsor evening lectures. Check local newspapers for current events.

Such preparation is useful, but the real impact occurs out there on the water with the whales. Seeing them is believing in them. ∎

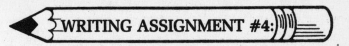

YOUR FAVORITE HAUNT

Go to your favorite haunt, a place you go to get away from it all. A corner of the bedroom, your summer mansion. In 500 to 750 words, tell why it's your favorite place. Show it. Make us feel it. But do it all without using the words, "I," "me," "my" and with hardly any other possessive pronouns. Use "you" or "one" occasionally, if you must. Make yourself a camera and tape recorder and show, don't tell.

WRITING BLIND

Because the eyes are so important to writing, play with your visual perceptibility in a variety of ways. Sit in a room you are very familiar with. Now close your eyes and recall as many objects as you can. Or sit in a room you are unfamiliar with and, without the aid of pen or paper, note as many things as you can. Leave the room and write down as many as you can recollect. For a real fun time, pair up with a trusted friend (who is also a writer), and one at a time lead each other *blindfolded* on a brief "trip" around the house or a park. After, write about the experience, drawing on all other senses except your eyes. You will discover how important seeing is to writing.

CHAPTER 4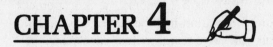

Stalking the Wild Story Idea: Where to Find It, How to Frame It

There are times when I am convinced that the idea is everything—even more important than the quality of the prose. Good writing can save a bad idea, but a good idea can sometimes save even bad writing. In fact, a good idea can inspire good writing. However, combine a bad writer and a bad idea and you've got the literary equivalent of junk food.

Editors are in desperate need of good and original ideas— places they have not covered before, or new angles on old places. They've got to put out their publications once a week or once a month. The Earth is finite; if Marco Polo hasn't been there, Horace Sutton has. This means editors must reapproach the same place from many perspectives and many times, since the most popular destinations are the ones about which people continuously want more information. Though Hawaii has been milked dry of story ideas, you can bet that every year newspaper travel sections and many magazines will find yet another angle on it—especially when you read that the number of people visiting Hawaii rose in 1987 to 5.7 million, a 3.3. percent increase over the record 5.6 million in 1986 (these are the kind of at-your-fingertips facts that drive travel writers' idea machines).

One could do worse than gain a reputation as an idea person. All writers—good, bad, or indifferent—rack their brains trying to come up with good ideas. As you hone your writing skills, also develop an understanding of the ingredients of a good idea.

One of the best ways to do this is to study newspaper travel sections and travel magazines, taking a close analytical look at the story ideas. You can do this quickly by examining the contents page. Break down the stories into categories. Is it an activity story, like horse-hiking in the Adirondacks? Is it a trend story, like "Loreto—the next Cancún?" Is it a round-up story: "Everything to do and see in Waco, Texas"? Is it about a museum, a gallery opening, a profile of a prominent figure? Is it based in North America, Europe, or the Pacific Basin?

How to Turn No Idea Into a Good Idea

So what *is* a "good idea"? Where does it come from? And what's the meaning of these terms editors are always bandying about: "angles," "focus," slant," "peg"?

To demonstrate what a good story idea is, for starters, let's consider what a story idea *isn't*. Someone has just returned from a trip to Thailand. He is enthralled by Thailand. He wants to write about Thailand.

"So what do you want to write about?" I ask.

"Oh," he replies," "just the whole thing, about how beautiful it is, from the beaches to the mountains . . . everything. I want to write about my whole experience there."

This gentleman has no idea of what he wants to write about, to put it politely.

There has to be a thread, a purpose, an angle, a focus. For example, the gentleman could examine one subject area: the dance of Thailand, or the food of Thailand, or a Thai museum, or a mountain retreat, or a festival. That would begin to give the story a slant.

But then, to refine the idea further, get even more particular. Consider a profile of the country's leading dancer, or write about a visit to a dance school, or attend an annual performance. Trace the geographic origins of a particular Thai herb to a village in the mountains. Then follow it to the best restaurant in Bangkok. Rate the newest restaurants in the city. Or write about a venerable costume maker in time for an upcoming festival. Or perhaps that mountain retreat has undergone renovation and is under new management. Now you've even got a timeliness—a news "peg," something that appeals to editors.

Keep shaping a story idea by sharpening the focus and tightening the frame. Writing a story from this defined point of view makes it easier to write and easier to read.

The key is to concentrate on one aspect. Too many beginning travel writers commit the same mistake as beginning novelists: They try to throw everything they know about the universe into their first effort. This is not necessary; in fact it's distracting. It's too much for the reader to absorb. It also forces you to write in too many directions at the same time in what usually turns out to be too little space.

What's the Story About?

The closet question silently crying out to be answered behind every story is: "What's the point?" Every story has to have a thrust, a reason for being. This is where "This is a story about" comes in again. If you can complete that sentence as

succinctly as possible, you probably know the point—the angle—
of the story and, more importantly, you will probably be able
to write about it better.

The "angle" or "peg" frequently turns up, not coincidentally,
in the keystone paragraph, that third, fourth, or fifth paragraph
following the lead to the story. Here is where you must, in a
manner of speaking, put your money where your mouth is.
Announce your point. Identify the angle. Tell us what the story
is about. State the obvious, but state it.

THIS IS A STORY ABOUT

Think of a travel story you'd like to write, preferably about
somewhere you've already been. Now, in one hundred words
or less, tell what the story is about, beginning with the words,
"This is a story about . . ." Write it in either a couple of
sentences or one long run-on humdinger. Take ten minutes at
most. Think of the story in its most generalized version. In
Hollywood, you're supposed to be able to sell your pitch in as
many words as those *TV Guide* blurbs; this is similar. It's good
practice and we will use it again when writing proposals in the
next chapter.

Is This a Good Story Idea for You?

You may come up with a great idea, but you may not be the
right one to write it. At least that's what some editors may tell
you—and for once they may be right. In order for a good idea
to be *good for you*, ask yourself two questions:

Why me? "There are many writers out there. Why should I

give this assignment to this alleged writer," asks the editor. The editor wants writers with expertise in the fields about which they are writing. He would love to be able to identify the author of the cover story as a leading authority on the subject—and one who can put two words together to boot! But, more to the point, the editor and his cherished reader can trust the facts. (*"It says right here he has a master's in medieval metaphors from Matchbox U!"*)

Even if you're not an authority, you can still claim authority by being very familiar with a place. (*"This is my eighth weekend getaway this year to Modesto, and my girlfriend's from there."*)

Practically speaking, for you the writer, familiarity with the general subject area or region means you won't have to do as much original research.

Why now? In a word, timeliness. Publications like to be contemporary. They like to be *now.* "The *New* Reno." They like to spot trends. They like to milk trends. They like to make trends where there are none. Australia became hot in the eighties, so Australia stories sold like crazy. In 1960 you couldn't have given away an Australia story.

"Why now?" may simply be that the peso has dropped. It may be the expansion of tourism facilities. An annual festival gives a story timeliness, as does the annual return of the monarch butterfly or the humpback whale.

A story that depends on a seasonal angle creates its own timeliness. For instance, every winter a great many North Americans think about where they can go to frolic in the sun, or loll on the deck of a cruise ship. So Caribbean island cruises in mid-winter have a built-in answer to "why now?" A story about Paris in April might be considered a seasonal story—if, that is, there was an editor romantic enough to consider such a cliche. (Stories whose timeliness depends on a season should be proposed to magazines at least six months in advance.)

These two questions become increasingly important at a later stage, when you write the requisite proposal to magazines (see Chapter Five).

Sources of Ideas

We are surrounded by ideas, if you know where to look and what to look for—and if you look with well-focused eyes. Some ideas come from your own life and travels, some from the journeys of friends. Others necessitate a little research. Still others are at your fingertips every Sunday morning.

"Borrowing" from the Media

I am an obsessive clipper. Esoteric little facts. Great quotes. Background pieces. Profiles. All stuffed into various expanding files with various headings. It's not exactly stealing we're talking about here, but collecting material: grist for the editorial mill. Some of these articles become the seed for an idea. Some remind me I ought to be thinking of a story about some place. I still have a clip entitled "Guatemala wooing the Americans," telling how the government tourism office is gearing up, with added facilities, flights, and good package deals. (They will also probably be adding to a budget to accommodate travel writers, which turns into possible free trips for known or assigned writers.)

I watch for offbeat ideas. In an article on where to stay in the Bay Area, there is mention of a bed and breakfast inn located in a tiny island lighthouse in the San Francisco Bay. I might propose a tightly focused piece on that B&B alone, written in a style that would be more detailed and evocative.

Reading the papers regularly also keeps you abreast of travel trends and up-and-coming destinations to add to your burgeoning files. In general, you should be familiar with the types of stories used by the publication you'd like to write for—if only to know what has already been covered.

I'm not opposed to adapting from one medium to another. I was once watching the local news on TV, which included a segment on weekend getaways in the Greater Bay Area. I saw some lucky reporter standing at cliffside somewhere near Eureka on the Northern California coast, talking about the history of the area. I grabbed a pen and started taking notes. Later, a proposal to *Women's World* on the famed Samoa Cook House resulted in an assignment to write about the whole coast from Eureka to San Francisco.

Talk to Returning Sojourners

When my friends come back from *wherever*, I drill them like war criminals for facts, reactions, opinions, recommendations, and other pertinent data, always on the prowl for new things I haven't heard about to do and see. Anything—food, night life, best beaches. Sometimes I will even pay for their lunch if they have let me pick their brains thoroughly. This drilling can annoy friends—but fear not, they will love you again when they find out that, based on one of their tips, you are on assignment in France inhabiting a gigantic villa on the Seine.

Ideas Under Your Nose

You may be on vacation and have no interest in writing about where you are. That's frequently when you get your best ideas, because they follow your instinctive interests. During my first trip to Hawaii I watched jealously for several days as helicopter tours of Kaui took off near my hotel. I resisted at first; it seemed like so much money for such a short thrill. I finally gave in, reached minor aerial orgasm, and came back

proposing a guide to Hawaiian helicopter tours for *Travel &
Leisure*—and got it!

Since editors want an expert and since you can always claim
expertise about where you live, look to thine own backyard for
ideas. That funky museum may house a great story. My first
assignment from *Travel & Leisure* came that way. Temporarily
ensconced in an eighteenth-century farmhouse situated on the
South Shore of Massachusetts between Boston and Cape Cod,
through the course of my daily wanderings I accidentally discovered a plethora of things to do, see, study, and enjoy.

Look around your area; there are stories. And don't forget:
In New York, where most travel magazine editors go to work
every day, Succasunna sounds pretty exotic (if not erotic) even
if it is in neighboring New Jersey. One man's hometown is
another's travel fantasy.

Part of the art is seeing your own environment with fresh
eyes. Most of us become so complacent about our day-to-day
surroundings that we assume everyone knows about them. I
stole an assignment out from under the noses of the local
writers in my first year living in the San Francisco Bay Area. I
wrote about the beaches of San Francisco for *Travel & Leisure*.
No native San Franciscan would have been so foolish as to
suggest that the city had any noticeable beach scene. But there
are beaches and they are well used, though not for catching
rays or swimming. Except if you're a seal.

Like a good salesman or jazz musician, turn an adversity into
a stroke of genius. For example, in that story I wrote on the
South Shore of Massachusetts, I used what appeared to be a
liability—that not too many people vacationed there—and sold
its lack of popularity as its attraction. If you spend two dismal
weeks stuck in a tropical rainy season in Trinidad, your story
idea could become: "Museums, indoor exhibits, and other things
to do and see when it rains in Trinidad."

Look for superlatives: the oldest, the newest, the only, the first, the last, the tallest, the westernmost tip of continental United States, the highest recorded wind velocity, the most rainfall, the deepest, the most remote, nearly extinct . . .

Talk to Photographers

Many professional photographers are walking idea machines, waiting to be plugged in to a writer. Align yourself early in the game with a photographer who thinks in terms of story ideas, in terms of storyboards, or images that tell a story. That's a good clue that he understands what a story is. He needs your ability to synthesize his bunch of pictures in verbal form. You need his vision and idea, and his contacts could lead you to publications. Editors likes writers who work with good photographers because they can already see a "story package" in the making. (See Chapter Ten for more on photography.)

Other Research

As helpful as any of the preceding tips may be, they may not be enough to generate an idea. In any case, they may not provide you with everything there is to know about a place. Luckily, however, there is a small army ready to barrage you with more materials than you thought imaginable. These are the tourism boards and other public information specialists whose life's goal is to have you turn their puffy PR pieces into legitimate travel prose. So use them; they love to be used.

Almost all compile so-called "press kits," which are packets full of press releases—everything from the history of the place to personnel, plus maps, guidebooks, schedules of festivals and other events, and ideas for stories. For the most part, these materials will be predictable. Wading through this stuff is like panning for gold, but every now and then something offbeat catches your interest. That's the idea that will separate your proposal from the thirty other writers who got the same press kit. Following are several types of organizations that make available information materials on countries and regions:

Government Tourist Offices In some cities they may be called Visitor and Convention Centers or Bureaus. Whether representing cities, states, or regions, these offices can supply information packets and press kits. Talk to the directors of these organizations when you have a particular angle in mind; if they're good at their job, they may rattle off half a dozen leads for you. These people love to help writers—that's their job. (See Appendix A.)

Embassies Generally not very helpful. They may refer you to their government tourist office or the public relations firm that represents them. The embassies are best when you need "official" verification for information like visas or shots, or for a quote from a high-ranking official.

Chambers of Commerce Though often too closely aligned with vested business interests to be objective in their assistance, town or regional chambers of commerce can inundate you with brochures and other tidbits of information. They also can lead you to prominent people in the business community and other sources.

Historical Societies Drop in on these archivists and you will be surprised how much you didn't know about the history of a region—and how interesting you could make it. Now if you can find a timely and contemporary linkup to some obscure historical item, building, date, or person, you've got a story.

Public Relations Firms Representing a region, a country, hotels, airlines, restaurants, and other travel industry accounts, they can give you the same press kits that the government tourist offices may send. The difference is these are the PR people who probably wrote the materials and so may be more familiar with them. They certainly better understand your needs, and can help "package" a story idea according to your editorial guidelines.

Travel Agent Newsletters and/or Publications Travel agents already conceive story ideas when they "package" a travel experience for their clients. They know what interests travelers. Publications like *Travelage East* (888 Seventh Ave., New York, NY 10106), *Travelage MidAmerica* (320 N. Michigan, Suite 701, Chicago, IL 60601), and *Travelage West* (100 Grant Ave., San Francisco, CA 94108) have information on package tours or theme trips that might be packaged as story ideas. The articles also are a good barometer of current trends in travel, perhaps suggesting a piece you may write. Sometimes a mere statistic can be the springboard for a story idea.

Travel and Tourism Organizations The Travel and Tourism Research Association (TTRA) is the international organization of travel research and marketing professionals, representing members from airlines, hotels, attractions, transportation, the media, and government tourism. Through membership ($35–$250), you get access to its Travel Reference Center, housed at the University of Colorado in Boulder, which contains America's largest collection of travel, tourism, and recreational data, articles, and other research (Executive Director, TTRA, P.O. Box 8066, Foothill Station, Salt Lake City, UT 84108).

The Travel Industry Association of America (TIA) represents the travel industry and provides forums and market programs, such as the Travel Industry National Conference & Marketing Showcase. It also publishes the TIA International Travel News Directory, which lists trade and consumer media contacts in over forty countries. (For membership and subscription information write: TIA, Two Lafayette Centre, 1133 21st St., N.W., Washington, DC 20036.)

Advertising Publications Ads and articles in *Ad Age* are a good way to keep abreast of travel trends. They report on travel publications' editorial shifts and transitions and also provide demographic information about magazine readership—all of which should give you clues to ideas, or at least parameters.

Travel Newsletters   These publications—some of which have short life spans—cater to the esoteric interests of their publishers, usually compulsive sorts who complain they cannot find hard-core reliable information about their pet penchant. They are great sources for the peripatetic writer on the prowl for unusual ideas. (See Appendix A.)

Magazine Indexes   Some magazines, *National Geographic* and *Travel & Leisure* among them, publish indexes of the articles they've printed. The titles suggest the kinds of stories a particular publication accepts. They may inspire similar ideas. Also, reading these indexes saves you from spending time thinking about an idea they've already covered. Sometimes a story that worked one place may be a new idea when given a different location. For example, I read in one magazine's index about a guide to the Los Angeles comedy club scene; I proposed a story about San Francisco comedy clubs to the same magazine and got the assignment. Some magazines charge a fee for the index, but it's well worth the price.

Magazine Newsletters   Some magazines publish their own newsletter. The American Automobile Association of Southern California's magazine, *Westways*, guides writers in a cheery fashion to what the publication is looking for and other tips. *Better Homes and Gardens* has been publishing a "Better Homes and Gardens Newsletter of Family Travels," geared toward advertisers, but again, useful for understanding who the magazine sees as its market, and the kinds of stories that will appeal to its readers. Write to magazines asking if they publish a newsletter for contributing writers.

Local Libraries and Librarians   You are entering a field of work where it is important to maintain very friendly relations with your local librarian and your local postal person (a very nice postman once saved a pair of plane tickets that I had inadvertently dropped into my corner mailbox). A research librarian could be crucial to your success if he can help dig out facts, references, books, and other data you had no idea existed.

Home Library Desperate for ideas? Browse through your bookshelves for ideas. Admit it—you've been looking for an excuse to thumb through some of those paperbacks you've schlepped from home to home. Maybe your old freshman geology book mentions a famous dig you just read an item about in a country you've been wanting to visit. Really scrounging? Read your encyclopedia for ideas.

CHAPTER 5

The Markets: Matching Ideas to Publications

The purpose of this book is to get you published, or published more. Let us assume that, having read to here, you can write well and know how to shape a decent idea. Now all you need is a place to get your story published. It is admittedly easier said than done, but, believe it or not, you are more than halfway there. There is no shortage of markets to be tapped. That's what this chapter is about.

The trick is to understand a particular publication's "editorial concept," as editors might say. That is, how it views the world and how it perceives itself in the context of that worldview. Looking through the lens of *Architectural Digest* you will no doubt see the world in an entirely different fashion than if you looked at it from the viewpoint of *Mother Earth News*.

Once you figure this out, decide if your story idea matches that publication's editorial viewpoint. Some people feel they write from a particular perspective—as well they should—but they refuse to budge from that stance if a magazine's point of view isn't consistent with their own. Those writers will not become widely published. If you want to write and sell your work, learn how to reshape your ideas so they fit into the editorial frames of many publications.

Ask yourself, "What is my point of view and which magazines most reflect it?" These should be the magazines to which you are naturally drawn. And because you and the editor share a sense of style and taste, you presumably won't have to twist yourself into an uncomfortable pretzel as a writer to reflect and represent that publication's perspective. This should also make it easier to write for such a magazine or newspaper.

OK, so you are a total devotee of *The New Yorker* and realistically have as much chance writing for it as you do winning the million-dollar lottery. One does need role models. But meanwhile, if you're looking for publications that will live up or down to your expectations, choose those that are more appropriately attainable from your writing level.

Become A Magazine Junkie

While you are searching, skim through everything you can find. Investigate what's out there, because your reading habits probably do not embrace all publications. In order to know where to sell your stories, you must know what's out there on the stands, so get familiar with the variety of markets for your writing. Also, if you want to score points with editors, being familiar with their product is essential. Among editors' top pet peeves are freelances who propose ideas that are completely inappropriate to their editorial needs ("Dear Freelance: We have never published, nor do we ever plan to publish, haiku poetry in *Semiconductor International*)."

I spent considerable and valuable time in the early part of my career standing at magazine racks. Hang out with the mags. Make a promise to yourself: Every time you pass a rack you will stop and pick up at least one magazine you've never read and study its contents. If you must, pay for the thing, take it home, and get out the microscope. There's a lot you can tell about a magazine when you scrutinize it closely.

Staring at the rack, you realize there are an intimidating number of magazines. And this is just what the mass public sees, the tip of the iceberg. But look at them: women's mags galore, health and fitness mags, astrology mags, garden mags, home mags, home and garden mags, architecture mags, and on and on.

Below the tip—not on the racks—are the in-flight magazines, the automobile, auto club, and oil company magazines, the railroad company magazines, the magazines of insurance companies, senior citizen groups, and nonprofit ecology groups, and a host of trade publications, to list a few. All are potential markets for the well-angled travel story.

Library magazine racks have the advantage of being indoors, surrounded by comfortable chairs, and you won't get the evil eye for thumbing through them. They also often house a wide assortment of magazines you may not find at your corner newsstand: foreign newspapers and magazines, professional journals, and others. Libraries stack back issues of these publications. Skim through a year's worth of any magazine and you will gain an education in publishing.

Expand the Travel Markets

As you may have noticed so far in this chapter, I have mentioned publications that you don't ordinarily think of as markets for travel stories. Broaden your definition of what markets are available for travel stories and you have just increased your chances of selling. In fact, almost every publication could be considered a travel market when you expand the definition of what a travel story is. For example, if you have just returned from a trip to Scotland, where the game of golf originated, you may be able to sell a story idea on a golf museum there to *PGA Magazine,* the Professional Golfer's Association magazine. If you've spent time in Japan studying flower arranging, consider *Horticulture* or any number of other garden magazines as potential markets for a travel piece based on that subject.

Anatomy of a Magazine

Here's how I examine a magazine to determine if I should or can write for it:

The Look

Is it a slick glossy or a tabloid? It will come as no surprise that the tabloid will usually pay less—unless you have exclusive pictures of Carly Simon's latest marriage on Martha's Vineyard. I get a feel for the publication by looking at its graphic design: its type style, use of headlines and photographs (are they color, black and white or mixed?), quality of paper. How the magazine looks—how it dresses itself—reveals how it positions itself. The better the overall quality of design, the "richer" it sees itself. Like some people, no matter how well some magazines dress themselves up in glossy color, they will be betrayed by unsophisticated prose. To gain a greater understanding of what makes for good graphics, I recommend a weekend seminar in graphic design offered at any adult education center.

The Names

I look at the contents page first, but like a thrifty eater reading a restaurant menu, I read from right to left. I look at the bylines first, in search of names I recognize. It's the nature of my schizophrenia that when I do see a familiar name, especially when it's someone I know, I am both elated and depressed. Elated because it means the magazine buys stories from people I consider my peers and therefore a potential market for me. Bummed out because the assignment went to that person and not me. This is even more unnerving when the story idea was one I had thought of but hadn't gotten around to proposing.

As I thumb through the magazine from front to back, I look at how prominently an author's name is displayed, visualizing my own on that page. You may think this egotistical of me, but when you have worked hard to produce a story, you too will want to make sure you are appropriately acknowledged for it. Besides, "clips" (copies of your writing samples) that showcase your name in big typography look better in your soon-to-be-burgeoning file of published works. Later, you will parlay these clips into more assignments.

As I look at bylines, I also look for what may be the single most important clue to whether this magazine is an appropriate market for me: the tiny, frequently italicized paragraph at the end of the story identifying the author. Sometimes called the "author's box" or "author ID," it informs me of the caliber of writer the publication uses. If I consistently see such author IDs as "Robert Redford is a well-known film star," or "Ronald Reagan is a former American President," I can assume this publication is buying glittery names and hoping great staff rewriters will craft comprehensible English from their manuscripts. If I see IDs like, "Isaac Asimov is the author of 279 books and wrote this while flossing his teeth," or "Daniel Goleman writes on behavior for *The New York Times*," I can surmise I am in a stiff competitive market and I may not yet be ready to submit proposals here. If I frequently read that "Karen Johnson is an associate editor of this magazine," I infer the magazine is written mostly in-house by staff writers and editors, and that the budget for freelance material is equivalent to what the publication spends on paper clips. If it says, "Ruth Miller is professor of linguistics at Harvard University," I know the publication emphasizes expertise and solid credentials for writing about a subject. But if I see, "Dorothy Drone is a freelance writer based in Highland Park, Illinois," this may indicate there is room for unrecognized (but not for long) garden variety freelance writers. If I find no author's ID, I cast a disparaging word against ingrates who call themselves editors, but if the magazine looks as though it pays well, I may consider writing for it anyway.

I also study the listing of staff members, known as the "masthead" or "staff box," first to see if there is someone designated as travel editor, then to see if I recognize any names. If I see the name of someone I have worked with, or know, or simply know of, I write it down; this person will be the one I write to when I am ready to submit ideas to the publication. If none are familiar, I still take note of the names because publishing is a volatile business; it's like musical chairs and you never know who will turn up where when the music stops. These are some of the people you hope to be dealing with at some time in the future, wherever they may work. I developed a personal and professional relationship with an editor whose career and friendship I followed from the San Francisco *Examiner* to *Parade* to *Signature* to *Look* to *Geo*. When he took a job in corporate communications on Wall Street, our friendship sort of petered out.

The Places

Are the travel stories local, regional, statewide, West Coast, North American, European, or worldwide? This informs me whether this magazine is going to send me to Hong Kong or to Hoboken. I also look at how the publication covers these places: general destination stories, seasonal angle, based on an event or annual festival, etc.

The Major Stories

The middle section of a magazine is called the "well." There are fewer ads in this section so that these features may be showcased, designed to include more full-page illustrations and better layouts. In the case of newspapers they will appear on the first page of the section. These are the plum assignments that usually command more money and demand better writing. These assignments often go to established writers who may already have developed a good working relationship with the publication. I study these particularly closely, observing bylines, lengths, and editorial treatment. Are they in first person or third? Are they written in a colorful narrative style or treated more academically? Do they include nut and bolts, like where to stay and sleep, with rates, in a separate smaller story (sometimes called a "sidebar" or "box") accompanying the major piece?

The Departments

In the front and back of the "book," as magazines are sometimes called within the publishing industry, or in various parts of the newspaper travel section, you'll find regular columns, departments, and sections. In magazines like *Family Circle* or *Esquire*, here is where you will find the travel department. These contain shorter stories (from 250 to 1,000 words), frequently more finely focused (a museum or upcoming event) than the features. Some are written by the same person every month. Some are written by a number of different contributors. Most editors suggest breaking into publications via these sections. Once you have proven yourself, then you are eligible for the major assignments. So get to know these sections well.

Advertisements, Classifieds

Some savvy travel writers, who understand what economists mean by "market-driven," take a close look at the quality of products advertised in the publication. If you see BMW and Gucci ads, you are in an upscale market and chances are your story idea about driving your Winnebago through Wisconsin will not be appreciated here. How about a private yacht trip through the Aegean Isles? Also, if you see many ads for cruises, chances are good there will be a need for cruise stories—such are the pressures that can be borne by influential advertisers.

Guidelines: For Closer Scrutiny

If you are interested in writing for a publication and want a clearer idea of whether your guidelines will meet its—or vice versa—write for "writer's guidelines." These outline what the publications expect and what you can expect financially. Written presumably by a top editor, guidelines should put into words what they're looking for (the "editorial concept"), listing story lengths, photo requirements, expense policies, and payment rates.

Good guidelines also offer a reader profile, based on a not-necessarily-rigorous demographic survey: "our reader," as they so endearingly put it, or a composite facsimile, by age, education, income, marital status, geographic location, possessions, travel habits. These are valuable data to an astute travel writer who can suggest things to do and see for people who fit that profile. I keep this information in mind when I am in the field on assignment: For example, "Would a fifty-five-year-old bachelor who lives in a trailer park outside Saugus, Massachusetts, truly find happiness skateboarding the back streets of Brooklyn in August?"

Here's a typical writer's guidelines from a Canadian magazine called *Touring and Travel*:

Writer's Guide

Tight, bright articles with practical, factual information will have the greatest appeal to readers. Most of the time they want to know how to do things. In Canada and the United States their average trip lasts a week to ten days. Every three or four years they head to Britain or Europe for three weeks to a month.

Make sure you have a good mental picture of our reader before you begin to write. They are very practical people. They read travel stories because they like to travel. They specifically tell us they don't like rambling writers.

Here are a few facts about our readers which will help you. Most travel with their family. On a weekend trip they don't like to spend more then $500. On a one-week motor tour they will try to keep below $800. However, they are prepared to spend twice that amount for a week when it means they fly-and-drive.

Every three or four years they like to take a trip abroad. This means they have worked hard to save enough money for a major holiday. Therefore, they expect tips that demonstrate the writer knows good value.

Story Outline

Editors prefer to work from story outlines. Either we write the outline or the writer suggests his own.

The outline should be clear and concise about the purpose of the story. It should identify the angle as well as briefly cover the key facts.

Some stories require pictures to make the story work. If specific pictures are critical to the story, make sure they are identified in the story outline.

Story Material

Our readers spend most of their travel time in Canada. Therefore, we will publish three or four Canadian articles in every issue. Not all of them will be major articles. Some will be short—only three or four paragraphs, and major stories will run about 1,500 words.

Also, the U.S. is a good neighbour who welcomes Canadians. Sunbelt stories from Florida and from California have great appeal in late fall and early winter. Spring and summer are the best times to travel the Northern States. Texas, the Carolinas, Virginia and Georgia are some of the favourite fall destinations.

Our readers seem to be food adventurers. Everything from good restaurants, fish markets or farmers' markets will catch their interest. Add two or three recipes to the story and you will have a real winner.

Our readers also want to know "when," "how much" and "how far." It is essential that we have the names of places, their rates and distances travelled, where applicable.

Style

A word about style—our magazine is positioned to be the travel authority to its readers, so stories should not generally be written in the first person.

Deadlines

If you plan to speculate a story or accept an assignment, make sure you know the deadline and meet it.

Pay Rate

An accepted story pays 20¢ per word on publication. An accepted transparency pays $15 on publication.

Remember

Editors do not wish to waste a writer's time. We prefer to work with a story outline to help you focus exactly on the story we need.

Special Kudos to Westways

As a commendable departure from traditional writer's guidelines, *Westways*, the bimonthly travel magazine of the southern California branch of AAA (Automobile Association of America), publishes *The Westways Writer*, a two-page monthly sheet with tips and updates on the magazine's need (P.O. Box 2890, Terminal Annex, Los Angeles, CA 90051). Among the kinds of advice and encouragement it offers: "One of our frequent contributors explained that whenever she goes out of town she takes the back roads; this has led her to small and interesting towns or little-known attractions, which in turn led to the sale of an article about these places." More practically, it suggests regions from which the magazine needs stories and, for photo submissions, it urges, "Please identify and describe your submitted photos as completely as possible. Editors have no way of knowing in advance the length of a given caption. They're often at the mercy of an art director's whims. It's better for the freelance to provide too much information than too little. Help your editor say something intelligent about your photo."

Good tips all. This is a freelance writer's delight. Every magazine that sends freelances form rejections should also send something like this. Besides being useful, it builds a sense of belonging for a writer and the magazine probably gains writers' allegiance in return.

Sources for Travel Writer's Markets

Writer's Markets (Writer's Digest Books, 9933 Alliance Rd., Cincinnati, OH 45242). In the beginning I spent many depressing nights looking through the four-hundred-page annual *Writer's Markets*. The book lists more than four thousand places to sell everything from filler copy to fiction. The problem is that travel markets are inconveniently dispersed under a variety of subject listings. Under "Trade, Technical, and Professional Journals" it lists such publications as *TravelAge West*, *ASTA Travel News*, and *The Travel Agent*, all geared for agents. "Travel, Camping and Trailer" includes more traditional travel markets, such as *Chevron USA*, *Travel & Leisure*, *Trailer Life*, and a number of state motor club publications. Such regional magazines as *Aloha* and *Yankee* are found in the "Regional City/State" section. Included are details of address, editor, phone, and circulation, approximate pay rates, and type of stories and photos editors want.

Pros and Cons: On the plus side, reading through *Writer's Markets* will give you a sense of what's out there, various pay rates and requirements. It's also helpful to see how editors describe their editorial needs. It provides a good overview of publishing. On the down side, however, don't depend on it for specifics like addresses, phone numbers, and names of editors. In fact, because of the vagaries of the publishing world and the lead time needed for publishing this annual book, there is no guarantee that by the time the book comes out any of the information will be accurate. So before you devote the next couple of weekends writing a poignant piece for *North American Hunter*, make sure it's still there by calling or writing.

Travel Writer's Markets (by Elaine O'Gara, Winterbourne Press, P.O. Box 7548, Berkeley, CA 94707). This ninety-page booklet, which is updated annually, is the answer for those too lazy to go to the library and sift through numerous volumes for addresses of newspapers and magazines. It includes over four hundred U.S., Canadian, and foreign magazines and newspapers (including a list of markets no longer accepting freelance), citing pay rates, travel editors to write to, types of photos used, contents, types of ads, sample story titles, and other particulars. This book is especially valuable for making multiple submissions to newspaper travel sections.

Travelwriter Marketletter (The Plaza Hotel, Room 1723, New York, NY 10019). In ten pages a month, editor Robert Scott Milne squeezes in tons of items on large and small editorial staff changes, new markets, free invitations to exotic and not-so-exotic destinations for assigned writers offered by PR firms, tour packagers, government tourism concerns, etc., plus book reviews and news on travel writing seminars, literary prizes and more.

Markets Abroad (Michael Sedge & Associates, 2460 Lexington Dr., Owosso, MI 48867). An eight-page quarterly that includes sections featuring countries and close-ups on magazines, and a "Noteworthy" section on writer's market reports. It also gives leads on other market sources: for instance, *Writer's Lifeline* (Box 1641, Cornwall, Ontario, K6H 5V6, Canada) is a specialized magazine listing Canadian markets for writers. Sedge also publishes *How to Double Your Income Through Foreign & Reprint Sales* ($10).

American Society of Journalists and Authors Newsletter (1501 Broadway, Suite 1907, New York, NY 10036). This thirty-two-page staple-job, published ten or eleven times a year, is for the eyes of ASJA's eight hundred members only. There are regional chapters in Washington, Chicago, San Francisco, western Massachusetts, and Florida. Membership requirements include being published eight times in the previous two years. Besides giving lonely writers a sense of belonging, membership

($120 annual dues, $50 one-time initiation) allows you access to various rights subcommittees, an annual directory of members, and the newsletter, which is sometimes worth the price of admission. Sections include "Market Monitor," updates on new or revamped magazines; "Pay check" and "Roundup," anonymous member reports on magazine fees. Anyone can order the *ASJA Handbook: A Writer' Guide to Ethical and Economic Issues* ($5.95) by writing Alexandra Cantor, executive secretary, at the above address.

Society of American Travel Writers (1120 Connecticut Ave., Suite 940, Washington, DC 20036). This nonprofit organization, founded in 1956, has about one thousand members with exclusionist tendencies. The entrance requirements are rather stringent. Applicants must be sponsored by two members. Freelancers must prove they have had work published in a variety of categories. Associate memberships are available for public relations types. The benefits include invitations to many places from travel organizations.

The Writer (The Writer, Inc., 120 Boylston St., Boston, MA 02116). This aging but stalwart monthly features mostly pseudo-inspirational essays and how-to articles, plus a section on special markets, which can be ordered separately at $2.50 a list. The May 1987 list features "Travel and In-flight" magazines. But others—like "Sports, Recreation and Outdoors" (January 1988) and "General Articles" (August 1987)—would be good travel markets as well.

Writer's Digest (Subscription: 205 W. Center St., Marion, OH 43305; Editorial: 1507 Dana Ave., Cincinnati, OH 45207). Another monthly magazine aimed at encouraging neophyte writers. Along with features like "12 Ways to Smash Writer's Block" and interview/profiles of celeb writers, "The Markets" department includes utilitarian items on new and changing markets with rates and requirements.

Metro Media (Public Relations Plus, Inc., Box 1197, New Milford. CT 06776; Tel.: 1-800-999-8448). A handy but expensive plastic-covered three-ringed booklet (updated annually) that lists daily and weekly newspapers, radio and TV stations, regional periodicals, bureaus, news services and syndicates. Newspaper listings include circulation and department heads. Double-check names by calling. This is useful for anyone who has anything to market. Available for California, New York City, and Metro New York (50-mile radius of Manhattan).

The Next Step: Matching Idea with Market

Once you have decided what to write and who to write for, make a list. In fact, make two lists. On one page list all your story ideas. There should be more than one idea, as no career is based on just one. The name of this game is ideas, so get used to generating lots of them.

On another page list all the magazines that you have deemed worthy of your prose and that you think may deem your prose worthy of them. Now match ideas to markets, listing ideas from the first page next to magazines (or newspapers) on the second. There may be some natural overlap, but that's OK because, as I will explain, the same idea may be written about in two entirely different ways without compromising the integrity of the idea—or ruining your reputation as a person who submits the same proposal to many different publications, a practice editors apparently do not savor but one that may be necessary in order to break even in this business.

I tend to focus on one particular magazine or newspaper to which I am trying to sell travel pieces. From my ongoing list of story ideas I take those ideas that would work for the magazine. I also see how the point of reference or angle of an idea might be reframed to fit my market better. As with writing itself, sometimes it's as simple as shifting the subject. For example, perhaps you want to write a story about Calistoga, the Napa Valley town known for its wine, its healing mineral water spas, and its glider planes. For *Food & Wine*, make the primary subject a new winery gaining lots of attention for its award-winning cabernet sauvignon. For *American Health* magazine, focus on the value of hydrotherapy. And for *Plane & Pilot* lead with an upcoming glider plane competition. All three versions of the story will be set against the same backdrop of the town of Calistoga, and each version might include a little on the other attractions of the town.

Marketing to Newspaper Travel Sections: The Spray Gun Approach

Most newspaper travel sections accept unsolicited freelance manuscripts only, and assign only rarely to writers with an established track record. In fact, many newspapers are prohibited by union regulations from assigning articles to freelances, a move presumably aimed at ensuring staff writers their jobs. Once you have developed a working relationship with an editor, she may "express extreme interest in using a good story like that . . ." or some such vague verbiage, which is tantamount to an "unassigned" (not in writing) assignment, meaning there's no legal obligation. In those cases, proceed to write the piece—but proceed with caution, knowing that any number of vagaries could make your efforts moot.

Almost every newspaper in the world has a Sunday travel section. All are potential markets for your freelance material. The problem is most pay a pittance—some as low as $25 for articles, the highest $250. What's a writer left to do? Here's one solution.

Write your high-quality tightly framed six hundred- to thousand-word article. Make a dozen copies. Pick out twelve newspapers in different parts of the country, so that they are in noncompeting markets (don't try this with newspapers that have national circulations, like *The New York Times* or *The Christian Science Monitor*).

Send a manuscript to each newspaper travel editor, with a cover letter that offers the enclosed "on a first-rights basis in your circulation area." That wording means you are not offering the same piece to the other daily across town or to any other paper that competes for the same market (for example, the *San Jose Mercury News* considers itself in competition with the *San Francisco Examiner/Chronicle*). The cover letter should also include a short paragraph about yourself.

As far as photographs are concerned, everyone agrees it's better to send black-and-white prints with the story but making prints at $3 or more per print becomes costly if you send to twelve or more papers at once. To save money, send either a high-quality photocopy of the print or mention that prints (or color slides) are available if the editor plans to use the story.

That's it. Now sit back and wait for the mailman to bring a check and a clip of your article as it appeared in these papers. Don't hold your breath, though. Some editors hold a story for months waiting for the opportune moment to use it. Don't bother calling, either. The phone bill cuts into the slim profits and won't necessarily help. If they don't plan to run it, they may throw away the manuscript without telling you (if you include a SASE, you'll get it back). If the editor of the *Chicago Tribune* returns the manuscript unused, send it immediately to the editor of the *Chicago Sun-Times*.

When this strategy works, you may sell the piece four or five times and make $400 or $500. If you keep careful records of who you send stories to, who's buying and who's not, you can establish your own little network of regular markets for your travel stories and develop ongoing relationships with several newspaper travel editors around the country.

Proposals and Query Letters: How to Get Assignments from Magazines

With magazines, the most widely accepted procedure requires you to write a proposal or query letter outlining your story idea and how you would go about writing it. As opposed to newspapers, most magazines dislike unsolicited manuscripts. Why? Imagine an editor at her desk. She is in an eternal state of deadline mania. When not, she rifles through mail and manuscripts. If she can dispense with something quickly, she will. If it needs more attention and she's got little to spare, she adds it to that ever-growing stack called "To Do."

The more important reason for a proposal is so that the editor can pick and choose the kinds of stories she would like and then participate in guiding the story to better fit her editorial needs. It means she can put her finger in the pie while it's being baked. When the editor is good, this serves to the writer's advantage.

For the sake of expedience alone, an editor would prefer a query letter. And, while it saves the editor time from reading a whole manuscript, it saves you from writing a whole manuscript, a longer prospect. A proposal is like test marketing your idea.

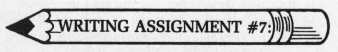

WRITING ASSIGNMENT #7:

"AND WHO ARE YOU?"

The Cheshire cat from *Alice in Wonderland* passed this one along to me. It is an exercise in ego and it is absolutely necessary if you want to market yourself. Write a five-line sentence or two describing yourself, as you would want your author's ID to read. Emphasize the area of expertise that gives you authority to write the piece. This will become a valuable paragraph in your proposal, telling the editor why she should assign you to write it (remember "Why me"?). It also sometimes helps assuage your own insecurity ("Who am I to write this?!") by seeing your credentials right there on paper. Fragile egos and falsely humble types need this kind of encouragement. Begin by writing: "I am a . . ." Now complete it.

How to Write a Proposal

Proposals are an art form all their own. The style of proposals is different from the style you are developing as a writer. A proposal is a sales pitch. It's fast-paced, almost businesslike, but at the same time more informal than a business letter. This is not necessarily the place to flex all your stylistic and literary muscles. It's OK to drop in an alliterative phrase or two, perhaps paint a pretty picture in words here and there, but your main aim is to outline what you want to write about, why it should be written about, and why you are most indubitably the one to write it.

As I mentioned previously, if you can convincingly answer two questions—"Why me?" and "Why now?"—you have a strong chance of getting an assignment.

A rule of thumb in writing proposals: Like all writing, less is better. My first proposals ran to two and three single-spaced pages. Now most are two-thirds of a page long. Earlier my insecurity made me overstate and oversell my ideas. Slowly I learned to economize on words, to use evocative imagery, and to hone the idea down to its basic elements—elements that will trigger an editor's interest.

When writing a proposal, keep in mind the lead-in sentence I suggested earlier: "This is a story about . . ." Somewhere your proposal should complete that sentence, though not necessarily in those exact words. Also, remember the keystone paragraph of your story, which may well appear in your proposal, explicitly stating the story's *raison d'etre*.

Writing proposals for the travel markets presents a particular problem: How do you write a good proposal without having been to the place you want to write about? To write a good proposal without going there first requires some preliminary research, garnering enough information to evoke the spirit of the place you want to write about. You may well already have most of what you need, collected earlier when you were hunting for and researching story ideas.

If you do need to do additional research, check out some books and maps at the library, make two or three calls, and photocopy some papers—remember that time is money and the clock is ticking. Gauge how much time you may need to collect enough information to strengthen your proposal and decide then and there whether the amount of time you put in is worth what you will get in return. Here, again, you can see the value of writing about places or subjects you already have some expertise about, since they will require less research.

By the way, any editor worth her weight in floppy disks can tell within two or three paragraphs whether you can write or not. That's why I write proposals with great care, sometimes spending half a day composing a tight letter. Given the busy life of an editor, this may be my one shot.

Sample Proposals: The Long and the Short of It

Here, as models of opposite ends of the coin, are two proposals I wrote that garnered assignments.

The first was written for *National Geographic*. This 1,500-word outline is far longer than anything I suggest you write, but I submit it for your perusal because it contains several of the points I've outlined here. It begins with a variation of "This is a story about . . ." It includes lots of visual description, especially important for a picture-oriented magazine like the *Geographic*. It and the next proposal refer to superlatives ("one of the last," "these guys offer the best"). It offers cameo profiles of several colorful local characters. It alludes to history and contemporary issues and gives a sense of how I might weave these all together. Finally, the real proof of the proposal's success is reflected by the fact that the lead for the story, as it appeared in the magazine, was drawn directly from this original outline. (See excerpts from the story in Chapter Three.)

"The Valley Is My Country"

Photographer Cary Wolinsky and I drove up to Maine last week to investigate a story about a group of hard-working, soft-hearted descendants of coastal Acadians who live literally at the geographic and cultural edge of two countries. These were people, we had heard, who maintain many of the old European traditions, who raise big families that keep close ties, and who still consider the Catholic church the center of their lives. And as if to confirm their isolation from the rest of society, they speak a Medieval dialect of French that linguists consider archaic.

But that, we discovered, is only part of a rich story possibility for National Geographic.

It turns out the community we encountered lies on both sides of the Upper Saint John River—which happens to be an international border. The approximately 60,000 people who live in the hundred-mile stretch from Grand Falls, New Brunswick, to Allagash, Maine, think of "the Valley" as a country apart from both Canada and the United States.

"The Valley is my country," beamed 19-year-old Patsy Bernier of Fort Kent, Maine, when we asked her to which country she felt stronger allegiance. Depending on which way you're going, Fort Kent is either the first or the last town on US Route 1, and Patsy sells either the first or last American hot dogs on Route 1 at a lunch stand a short stone's throw from the international customs house.

The gracefully flowing river winds its way through the fertile valley, irrigating the land and making it rich for the main crop, potatoes. Using a method their ancestors brought from France, farmers have divided the plots of land into thin parcels leading away from the river so that each has access to both the water and the hillside woodlands. They are called "suspender farms," and when viewed from the air make the valley seem bound in green strips of ribbon.

A great portion of the names that sprinkle the Valley phone book—LeBlank, Daigle, Cyr, Hebert, Duperre, Fournier—are direct descendants of the 22 original families that made their way to this remote terminus of the Saint John River when the tyrannical British dispersed the French Acadians from their coastal homesteads in Le Grand Derangement of 1755.

The Ashburton-Webster Treaty of 1842, which established the Upper Saint John River as the boundary between the United States and Canada, effectively made many of those families international relatives. Today, it is not uncommon for an American man to have Canadian in-laws, or for brothers and sisters to salute different flags. To the people of the valley, though, the international border is nothing more than a river they nonchalantly cross. The expression in the valley is "going across," or "he lives across." Many live on one side and work on the other. A fact that demonstrates the interconnected nature of the two sides is that the four valley bridges linking Canada to the United States account for the third largest volume of cross-border traffic along the whole of the American-Canadian line.

Another example of international cooperation is the Fraser Paper Mill, the valley's largest industry. A large pipe crosses the river, pumping pulp from a mill on the Canadian side to the paper-producing mill on the American side. We couldn't help but think of the pipe as a giant international umbilical cord. One more example: half of the members of the Edmundston (New Brunswick) Republicans baseball team are Americans.

* * *

"The Franco-Americans of Northern Maine remain among the least assimilated ethnic groups in the United States. The physical remoteness and cultural isolation of the Saint John Valley from the mainstream of American culture, the rural environment, an inadequate and unsympathetic educational system which bred traditional illiteracy, were all contributory factors in the preservation of a vast and remarkably unspoiled folklore."

That analysis comes from a man who has entrenched himself in the cultural traditions of the valley. Roger Paradis, professor of history at the University of Maine's Fort Kent campus, and a native of the valley, has taken on the ambitious project of collecting the folklore of the region before 20th Century America creeps its way up Route 1 and homogenizes this colorful culture into the American melting pot. He has already accumulated one of the largest collections of Acadian folklore known: tales, songs, myths, proverbs, herbal remedies, poems about mythical lumberjacks and woodsmen, wooden toys and trinkets, quiltwork and needlepoint, sculpture and paintings. And the valley is still as rich with this heretofore untapped natural resource as it is with potatoes.

The strong sense of pride in heritage pervades these people. The town of Van Buren is busy building a full-size replica of an 18th Century Acadian village, and every summer the town sponsors a fair called "Heritage Vivant," Living Heritage, to display their culture. This summer, with the Bicentennial as an excuse, the people plan to pull out all the stops and organize a valley-wide festival to show off their songs, dances, costumes and their unique culinary arts (the local chicken stew is outstanding; the buckwheat pancakes, "ployes," and many other recipes are found nowhere else in the world). By the way, mention Longfellow's "Evangeline" and you're bound to make quick friends.

More than any other cultural indicator, language reflects a people. The natives of the Upper Saint John Valley—the region is also called le Madawaska—have held on to a dialect whose vocabulary, phonetics and syntax relate directly to the 16th and 17th Century dialect spoken south of the Loire River in France. Walter Lichtenstein, a linguist specializing in Medieval French, couldn't believe his ears when he came to this area to study the language. "It is remarkable the dialect has stayed this pure, considering the possibilities of influence from the Quebec French or the Anglican English," he noted. A federally-funded Title VII bilingual studies program, in its sixth year in the valley, is aimed at ensuring this oral treasure is not made obsolete.

*   *   *

The first thing we noticed driving into the area was that the biggest, most impressive buildings in the valley are the ornately decorated Catholic churches and, indeed, they are still very much a focal point. As one person we talked to said, "There is only one traffic jam around here, and it's on Sunday." Other distinctive architectural features we noticed along the way were the century-old barns and houses with roofs and other design touches reflecting the French influence; also the traditional wooden potato houses dotting the fields.

We got a sense of genealogical engrossment from Monsignor Ernest Lang, who lives in St. Basile on the Canadian side. The Rev. Lang is 77 years old, but he has the sparkling eyes of a man 20 years his junior. As a sort of post-retirement hobby, he has put together an eight-volume genealogy of the entire valley, going back in some cases almost 300 years to trace the origins of a family.

We talked with a potato farmer and discussed the big "issue": whether potatoes can keep fresher longer in the old-style wooden potato houses or the more modern metal Quonset huts. As the potato harvest goes in this region, so goes the economy. Everyone knows exactly how much money a bushel gets.

We stopped along the road and found Eudore Nadeau milking his cows—by hand—in his 100-year-old classic barn. We marvelled at the beams and walls. Eudore, amused at our curiosity, his big round cheeks red as beets, shouted: "Oh, it's been standing so long it doesn't know how to do anything else."

We chatted with "Whitey" Rahrig, publisher of the only English-speaking weekly paper in the valley. Whitey is a native of Ohio who came up to work on his brother's newspaper in 1960 and loved the people and the pace so much he never left. We understood why.

The following proposal was offered to thirty or so publications. It was accepted by the Living Section of *The New York Times*. It is succinct—less than two hundred words long—but ably outlines what the story is about and gives a flavor of my tone of voice.

"Down the Salmon River in Upscale Style"

On July 16 I will be joining the Salmon River Outfitters on a five-day river rafting trip down the second deepest gorge in North America, traversing 400 miles of white water through the largest wilderness area in the Lower 48. But no ordinary man's Deliverance, this. We go quite civilized, served the finest in gourmet cuisine at each night's stop. *Bon Appetit* and *Sunset*, among others, have lauded chef/guide Steven Shephard's fresh salmon with wild rice, mushroom quiche, shish kebab, salmon-stuffed tomatoes, chicken enchilada, fresh baked breads, banana nut pancakes ... need I go on? Of the many outfitters I've heard of that guide trips down rivers, these guys offer the best. They also offer such specialty trips as "Idaho Plant and Flower Identification," "Photography Workshop," "Astronomy Interpretation," and (how could we do without?) "California Wine Tasting."

I can craft a 1500-word piece that revels in both the pristine wilderness and the poached salmon. I would like to know with a quick phone call response of interest in assigning the piece before I go so I can better plan how to cover it. Also since I have photographed for *Travel & Leisure* and other publications, it would be good to discuss picture requirements, as I would be glad to contribute either black and white or color.

What to Include in Travel Proposals

- Convince an editor of why she should run this story and why now.
- Emphasize the "do and see" attractions (because, as the editor of an upscale travel magazine once told me, "even the idle rich aren't idle").
- Give a very brief physical description of the place and its geographic location.
- Who will like this place and why will it be of particular interest to this publication's readers?
- Map out your strategy for writing the story, how you'll execute it, including who you may quote, whether you would write it in first or third person, with humor or seriously, as a chronological narrative or diary entry formula, whether you plan to include a "box" with nuts-and-bolts type of information. Tell how long the story would be in number of words, and when you plan to deliver it.
- Do you anticipate incurring any expenses that you'd like the publication to pick up? It's worth asking.
- Who are you and why should the editor assign you to write the story?
- Clips. This is high-tech jargon for photocopies of your published articles or, if you are feeling magnanimous and can spare it, the actual article clipped from the newspaper or magazine. To enhance the presentation of your work, cut the story cleanly from the page (excluding ads, etc.). To make it look better, at the top of the page paste the section title with the publication's name and date, with your story under it. Presentation counts in this field (memorable letterheads are worth the investment). It's best to include clips that represent the style you plan to use in writing the piece, or demonstrate your knowledge of the subject matter. (No matter how well received, professional papers and theses are *not* recommended.) To those who

worry that a good piece they wrote "only appeared in my neighborhood weekly," I say if your writing's good, that's the selling point; where it's published might not be so important.

- A (brief) word about availability of photographs. This will be covered in more detail in Chapter Ten, but for now you should mention in your proposal whether you are interested in taking photographs to accompany the story, whether you know or work with a professional photographer who is interested, or any other sources for pictures.

Two Types of Proposal Marketing Strategies

There are as many ways to write a proposal as there are styles of writing. Here are two approaches that work:

The Hit-'Em-With-Your-Best-Shot All-in-One Approach

This is advisable for writers who may not yet have solid samples of published work to submit with their proposal. In that case, you must demonstrate your ability to write from the very start. Begin your letter with an attention-getting lead, as though you were actually writing the lead to the story and continue for two paragraphs. This "mock lead" will be admittedly tentative, since it will be based on a sketchy sense of how you *might* write the story. Then continue with a transition like, "this is how I would begin a story about . . ." Of course, the drawback here is that since writing the lead is the hardest part of writing any piece, you have your work cut out for you. Console yourself by knowing that you may have saved yourself some hard work later on when you use the same lead in your final draft.

The See-Attached Approach

This is the approach I prefer, and not just because I have a sample of published work to show with my proposal. This method involves a cover letter and a separate page for each proposal, plus a variety of appropriate clips.

The cover letter simply states that you are "a professional freelance writer"—*or whatever*—"and would like to propose the enclosed story idea about whale watching tours of the Hawaiian Islands," for example. In the second paragraph, you might elaborate on your credentials, if they aid your case. Or you might briefly detail why this story idea is so well suited for this publication.

Keeping the cover letter and proposals separate allows the editor to detach the proposal so that it can get passed around to other editors who will have an opportunity to throw in their two cents on whether the writer should be assigned. It may be photocopied and passed out at an editorial conference attended by top editors, who comment on it.

This approach looks and reads cleaner as well. You can deal with each idea separately and, like modular furniture, it's flexible too. In other words, you can write up your ideas on separate pages and then insert them with others you think appropriate for the particular publication you have in mind.

An important by-the-way: Don't forget to include your name, address, and telephone number on *all* pieces of correspondence.

Include a Number of Proposals

Some writers feel as though editors will consider them wishy-washy if they submit more than one proposal. They say, "The editor will think I'm not that committed to any particular idea." Quite the contrary. Editors love to work with writers who can come up with more and more ideas. Flood them with ideas. Include about three ideas per submission. My theory is that this is my precious moment with an editor. I may not get another chance for a while. Frankly, chances are not great that any single idea will be assigned, but at least you improve your odds by offering a choice from among several ideas.

Multiple (or Simultaneous) Submissions: Pros and Cons

There is the "party line" on this issue and there is the survivalist's rationale. Multiple submissions—offering your idea to a number of publications simultaneously—is frowned upon by editors. They lament, "Why should I spend my valuable time reading a proposal, deciding with other editors whether to assign you to write this piece, when you have already accepted the assignment from our competitor? Where's your loyalty, lad?" And we should commiserate with them

Yet, ideas are fleeting things. And because it's difficult to lay claim or declare propriety to ideas, they are up for grabs. So timing is a factor. If writers submit their ideas to publications one at a time, they may wait up to a month or more for what turns out to be a rejection anyway. By that time, their idea may be stale or stolen.

Also, you have no idea about other variables that may make your idea unacceptable—the magazine just assigned that same story, the magazine's biggest advertiser forbids them from running that kind of story, the editor woke up on the wrong side of his water bed.

The compromise is to submit simultaneously to noncompeting markets. Noncompeting means the publications' readership don't overlap geographically (like *Yankee* [New England] and *The Bay Guardian* [northern California]) or compete for the same interest group (*Field and Stream* and *Ladies' Home Journal*). You wouldn't submit the same idea to *Esquire* and *Gentlemen's Quarterly*.

If you submit ideas simultaneously to noncompeting markets, should you tell them? My answer is this litmus test: If I even have to ask myself if I should tell, then I probably shouldn't be submitting it to this publication.

Whom to Send It to

Of course, when you are on speaking terms with someone on the staff, send the proposal to that person. If nepotism isn't in your blood, send it to either the managing editor, the articles editor, or the editor of the department you want to write for (travel, health, fashion, etc.).

If you do know an editor, it certainly helps. But don't give up if you don't. "Having a friend in the biz" is not essential; if your proposal or manuscript is good, it will get rerouted to the right person. Eventually. My first sale to *The New York Times* came when I wrongly sent an idea to the food writer, who has no authority to assign stories. She passed it along to the Living editor, albeit by a long and circuitous route. The editor called me well after I had already returned from the trip and had planned to write the piece for another publication. Wisely, I turned down the opportunity to write it for the *Oakland Tribune* and did it instead for the *Times*.

Waiting is the Hardest Part

Time out for a little creative visualization: Picture an editor in her crowded office in New York. It's not a pretty picture. Your missive arrives by mail three or four days after you sent it. The letter takes another day to get to her desk. Now it sits there, getting shuffled from one pile to the next, until it finally gets read two weeks after you sent it. She broods about it for a weekend and Monday morning passes it on to another editor who can approve the assignment. Another week goes by. And so it goes . . .

A month later you get a form note of rejection, with no feedback at all. A certain paranoia begins to set in. Two weeks later, out of the blue, you get a call from an interested editor who assigns you the piece. Elation takes over. Such is the manic life of a freelance.

If you haven't heard back from a publication after four or five weeks, something is amiss in the system and you are entitled to inquire what's up. A brief note or phone call may be in order, as long as your position is that you are just checking to see if the proposal arrived, if the editor had considered it, and whether she could inform you of her decision, as you'd like to submit it elsewhere otherwise. If an editor senses hostility or belliger-ence in your voice, you'll probably be treated in kind. But sometimes the little jog of memory guilt-trips them just enough to "get to it right away." And sometimes—golden opportunity!—she says, "Remind me of the idea," at which point you can jump right into your song and dance, retelling the idea with as much enthusiasm as you can muster and as succinctly as possible.

Is it necessary to include a self-addressed stamped envelope (SASE) with your submission? Most publications do ask that. If you don't include one, you may not get back your clips and proposals. Which is no great loss if you have kept copies of everything—*which you should*. If you provide no return-mail envelope, a happy consequence may be that the editor files your writing samples and "rediscovers" you months (years?) later. If you positively want your materials back, include the SASE.

You Got the Assignment! Now What?

If there is a Patron Saint of the Freelance Travel Writer and He or She is smiling upon you, then after a reasonable amount of time you will receive a letter of assignment. Keep this; file it with the folder of research you have kept. It is, first and foremost, your contract in writing and will serve as a legal document should there be any difference of opinion on the financial agreement between you and the publication.

The letter from the editor should stipulate your fee for the story and photographs (if you've agreed to take them), your deadline, the length of the story, and the arrangement regarding expenses.

Besides that, good editors will include some editorial guidelines, putting into words their interpretation of your proposal and how they would like you to go about making your idea work for them. In the best of all possible worlds, their vision matches yours. There are times, however, they may want you to take a different slant than you had in mind. If it doesn't compromise your integrity too much, make the adjustment.

For example, I proposed a story on the California ghost town of Bodie. *Diversion* magazine responded by assigning me to write a wrap-up story of ghost towns of the West. In her letter of assignment the editor wrote:

Dear Perry Garfinkel,

I am writing to assign you an article of approximately 2000 words on "Ghost Towns" for our January issue. The piece will be due on September 1 and will be used as a black and white feature (if your pictures are wonderful in color, there's a possibility of turning it into a color feature); upon publication, we will pay you $500 plus $100 for expenses.

The piece will discuss the phenomenon of ghost towns in historical as well as touristic terms: what constitutes a ghost town, where they are, how many exist today, why, and how, the towns "died," which ones are popular tourist attractions and why, the tours one can take, and any interesting, funny, or offbeat anecdotes about them. The piece can be evocative, a kind of spirit-of-America, as well as an informative tourist piece—it might open with a mood-setting description of one of the towns and spin off into history and travel facts from there. I'm sending you the two most recent editions of the magazine, as well as our September 1981 issue because it contains an article on Ellis Island, somewhat in the spirit of your piece. I'm also enclosing a Xerox of the *Wall Street Journal* article on ghost towns—please forgive the bizarre Xerox job.

Feel free to call with questions. I'm delighted you'll be doing the article—it should be very interesting—and I look forward to working with you.

Sincerely,

It is never easy to combine the nuts-and-bolts of a so-called service piece with an evocative slice-of-life feel. But I managed. (See Chapter Three for how I started the story.)

When thinking about writing your story, refer back to the editor's suggestions in the letter of assignment. They will be very helpful in keeping you on target.

With this valuable letter of assignment, now it's time to do your thing. Maybe this will require you to fly to Pago Pago—or walk to the local park. In either case, you are ready to hit the road, and the next chapter will guide you in the field on assignment.

To give the editor confidence, send a quick note acknowledging receipt of the letter and reasserting your plans for completing the story on time. If you have questions, call the editor and ask. That's professional and it's better than making a mistake that costs you time and money.

You Didn't Get the Assignment! Now What?

If the gods are not in your corner you may get a seemingly curt letter of rejection, all the more insulting if it's a standard form letter. "Your story does not fit our editorial needs at this time," and other impersonal non sequiturs tell you nothing. So forget them. Move on. Don't feel dejected or rejected. Just submit your idea elsewhere until you do get some authentic feedback. There are too many reasons that your story may have been rejected—many of them having nothing to do with the quality of your idea or your writing—for you to give up.

If, however, you get a letter from an editor turning down your particular idea but encouraging you to submit other ideas, do so. A letter that says, "Thanks for the well-worded proposal and though we will pass on this idea, try us again," lets me know I have a foot in the door. This invites a continuing correspondence that may turn into an assignment down the road. Do not underestimate the power of this ongoing relationship. After all, don't serious commitments require more than a good opening line on a first date? Imagine your first proposal as the first call made by a salesperson. What you are doing is introducing yourself. Maybe this line of ideas is not what they're looking for, but the next time at least you won't have to start from scratch introducing yourself all over again.

CHAPTER 6

Being There: On Assignment

First an ode to serendipity. To quote the Scottish bard Robert Burns, "The best laid plans aft gay astray." And, to recall Steinbeck's words from earlier: "Tour masters, schedules, reservations, brass-bound and inevitable, dash themselves to wreckage on the personality of the trip."

Sometimes, as in jazz, the best trips evolve out of mistakes. These are the vagaries of vacationing that add adventure to every outing. No matter how carefully you plan your trip, don't take it all too seriously. If you assume things will go wrong, you won't be disappointed—and you may be pleasantly surprised. There may be A Greater Plan at work.

The decision to travel somewhere in order to write about it, whether assigned or not, should set into motion a chain of reactions. The first is to picture yourself a short period from now basking in the glory of some peak travel moment. You do this just to whet your appetite and to whip your motivation. You will need it, for now begins what would seem to be the easiest part of travel writing but one that can make or break your whole experience, not to mention blow the story (and a lot of money as well).

As you are picturing yourself in traveler's nirvana, also picture yourself in traveler's purgatory. It can happen, as any true traveler can attest. Much of your preparation should be in anticipation of everything you will need in either locale.

In short, preparing to travel to research a story requires the same preparation as any trip. However, as a travel writer with editors waiting and responsibilities to fulfill and with quite possibly only one shot at being in some location, there is a particular pressure on you, so it's even more important to plan carefully. Do as much advance work as possible, making sure every detail of your and your story's needs will be met without great travail. This means some serious plotting. The more advance planning you do before you travel, the less time you will waste on the road.

Setting Up the Trip

When planning your journey, there are two things you should remember to take care of at all times: yourself and your story—and often you must be willing to put the latter before the former. In terms of yourself, as with all travel, keep your body healthy. It's the only one you've got and you can't afford to be ill while working on an assignment in some godforsaken luxury Caribbean resort hotel. Bring pills and ointments, and have major periodontal work completed well before departure. The rest of your attention should focus on getting as much information for your story as possible.

Determine Your Itinerary

At this important stage you can give shape and direction to your story. As you review the preliminary research you have presumably already amassed, decide what you want to do and see—emphasize *do* and *see*—in the amount of time you have allotted for the visit. Include those things that relate specifically to your story, of course, but also leave time to visit places or events that will give historical backdrop and a greater picture of the place.

While you are still at home, get out the map and become as intimate with your destination as possible. Be realistic about how much you can cram into one day. A good rule of thumb: Plan three "coverages" a day—one in the morning, one in the afternoon (optional in very hot climates), and one at night. Make sure travel connections are possible and that departure and arrival schedules work with your itinerary. Make as many advance reservations as possible.

When setting up your itinerary, plan to visit what's new and what's old. Visit what's odd and what's standard tourist fare. Cover both sides of the spectrum to cover your behind.

Even if you're not planning to write about it, see the thing that the region is most famous for—and if you don't know what it is, find out. Follow that thing through from its creation to its use. For example, Mazatlán, Mexico, was known as the second-leading exporter of shrimp when I covered it. In one long day, I was at the docks at dawn, watching shrimp come off the boats and talking to fishermen. Later I was at the fish market, watching it sold and interviewing a spokesman for the shrimp industry. By afternoon I was in the kitchen of a top restaurant getting recipes from the chef. Then, as just reward, from poolside at my hotel I ordered shrimp cocktails from the dining room. All the while I took notes and photographs.

How Long Should You Plan to Stay on Location?

The non-answer is: It all depends. The practical answer is: As long as you can afford to stay. The correct answer is: As long as it takes you to get the story you need.

Logically one would think that more time is better, since the longer you stay the more material and ambience you will collect. But this does not necessarily hold true. There is such a thing as too much of a good thing, for after a while some destinations will lose their sparkle and you will know too much for your own good. This information overload will make writing about the place difficult and lead to cumbersome prose.

On the other hand, I have spent from five weeks to three months in some places while researching a story and marinating in the culture. The resulting stories resonated with an authenticity that came from being on the inside. But that was the kind of piece the magazines wanted.

Some destinations do not need that kind of portrayal, however, and some publications would prefer a fast-paced story that introduces a destination to a first-time visitor. Since many travelers may only spend three to five days there, the travel writer should do the same, simulating the "real traveler's" experience. In that amount of time you should be able to cover the necessities if you waste no time (remember you may have to do and see more than the average traveler so that you can save him time).

Timing Is Everything

There is no more frustrating experience than arriving at a museum or a park to discover it just closed—for the next three months. Always check opening and closing hours, for yourself and for your reader (include the information in your story as well). Know the days business offices are closed.

Also carefully consider the time of year. Is it off-season,

when everything is closed? (I visited Austria once between ski season and the summer season when the only action was centered around the local cafe.) Is it the peak season, when reservations will be nearly impossible and lines imposing? Is it foliage season? Is the scarlet ibis, Trinidad's national bird, out of town on its annual migration just when you plan to be there? Is there a national holiday when all businesses will be closed or preoccupied with the upcoming festivals and parades? What *are* the business hours and is the Sabbath celebrated on Saturday, as in Israel, when everything comes to a standstill from Friday afternoon to late Saturday night?

Get Your Paperwork Out of the Way

Find out all the requirements for your travel plans: passport, visa, tourism card, birth certificate, student ID (for student discounts), international driver's license, etc. The local embassy usually knows what you'll need and where to get it. Also check to see what inoculations are required and get them, too. Finally, check on the current currency exchange rate, and buy enough of the foreign currency before you go to get you through the first day or two once there. Traveler's checks are also recommended.

Travel Agents: Pros and Cons

Those who have hitherto left all this to travel agents, welcome to working-class travel. Most travel writers' itineraries are so intricate that they are better off making all travel arrangements themselves. It also gives you more familiarity with the material. Setting up accommodations yourself enables you to ask a hotel representative lots of "journalistic" questions that a travel agent might not ask. Familiarity with all aspects of the travel experience gives your writing a hands-on feeling.

Some travel agents naturally have a travel writer's mind-set, since they are accustomed to planning and packaging trips, coming up with things to do and see, places to stay and eat. But for the most part, they seem too plugged into packages, tours, and accommodations that anyone can find in brochures and other promotional materials. They deal with too many people who seek the predictable, safe escape—which is, regrettably, the way too many people travel. If, however, you regularly work through one agent who gets to know you and what kinds of unusual things you're in search of as a travel writer, a travel agent may be helpful.

Traveling Solo or with a Group Tour: Pros and Cons

Most group tours provide the advantage of someone else taking care of all the tiny details and connections. If you have the opportunity to travel on a "press junket" with a group of other travel writers, journalists, and perhaps others in the tourism industry, you may feel somewhat constricted by someone else's timetable, Some tour leaders are more willing to accommodate a particular writer's interest if possible.

If you think traveling with a bunch of other travel writers is glamorous, filled with long romantic evenings swapping exotic travel adventures, think again. Long-time travel writers working for newspapers, for instance, are a somewhat jaded crowd, not easily impressed. They frequently compare (unfavorably) where they are with where they were last week. Except for the occasional "networking" with a travel editor, it is an experience worth foregoing, in my estimation.

Should You Travel with a Companion (AKA Significant Other)?

This depends on the companion. In the best of situations, your traveling mate is your best friend and can flow with the vagaries of your work. If your companion is ready to play "travel writer on assignment" with you, you're both in for a fun if flexible time. Two heads—and bodies—are better than one; together you can strategize optimal itineraries, or take quick surveys (of each other) on whether people would enjoy this museum or that restaurant. You can divide the territory, covering different parts of town for a morning and reporting to each other at lunch.

On the other hand, there are times when you can travel faster solo. There are also times when it was *because* you were traveling alone that you gained access to an encounter or experience. With one less collaborator, you are free to go at your own pace. One thing to bear in mind for those who may be seeking complimentary accommodations and air fares: Unless you can prove your mate truly *is* your photographer, your significant other pays his or her own way.

Apprise Appropriate Authorities

Set up interviews in advance when possible. It would be a shame to arrive only to discover that a prime source or government official is on vacation, or too booked to see you. Write ahead, including a sample of your work and perhaps the publication you're working for, anything to give yourself some clout and credibility.

If you are going to ask for financial assistance from hotels, airlines, public relations representatives, government tourist boards, contact these people as soon as you have an assignment in writing. Most will want to see the letter before they try to help. (More on that in Chapter Seven.)

They will want to know your itinerary, which will not be easy to tell since at the same time you will be contacting everybody. If such-and-such hotel can provide a complimentary room only on such-and-such dates, then your plans may have to revolve around theirs. Since many airlines have "blackout" periods, when free fares for travel writers are prohibited, you are also at the mercy of their schedules. Then, what if the government tourist board can only offer a free car on another date? And so on. These are the times when you'll wish you had a travel agent making the arrangements, but they are also exactly the times when you realize only you can do it, since your needs are so specialized. Just try to keep your priorities in order—that is, first consider what you will need to complete the research for your story.

What to Bring

Writing Tools

The first and most important thing for a writer to bring is everything he will need to write: a stash of pens, pencils, and paper. I recommend the thin (four inches by eight inches) reporter's notebooks that fit into jacket or pants pockets; they make note-taking easier (write Portage Newspaper Supply, P.O. Box 5500, Akron, OH 44313 for order forms, minimum orders of six dozen). Also bring yellow thin-lined legal pads because their cardboard backing serves as a built-in writing surface during occasional attempts to write on the road.

Conspicuously absent from this discussion is a typewriter. Rarely will you see a writer traveling with his typewriter these days, even the small portables. On the road, typewriter junkies can rent one or ask to use the hotel or business's office typewriter off hours. Nowadays, the progressive writer on the road is likely to have a six- to ten-pound portable battery-operated laptop computer, anything from the cheap Radio Shacks up to the highly recommended versions by Toshiba (See Chapter Nine for a look into travel writing's future.)

A Tape Recorder

Record interviews with people, record your own "field notes," street sounds, bells, or kids singing. Also bring plenty of extra batteries so that you don't have to look for them at a local shop. Same for extra blank tapes: bring as many as you think you'll need plus a few more (the 90- to 120-minute cassettes are best, since you don't have to change the tape as frequently). And while you're thinking about tapes, bring a couple of your favorite music tapes, especially valuable when homesickness hits hard. Unless you're using a professional field recorder to pick up quality sound and voice for future radio presentations, small recorders are just fine. For interviews on the road I've been using an Aiwa TP-27 cassette recorder, which also features a good pause switch for transcribing. It's 3.3 inches by 4.5 inches and costs about $125.

A Camera

No matter what quality and even if you don't plan to try to sell your pictures, bring a camera. As part of your research as a writer, shoot pictures just to remind yourself of what locations look like. Bring as many rolls of film as you need, then bring several more. My camera is a beat-up, altogether abused 1974 Nikkormat 35-mm single lens reflex. I have two filters (UV and polarizing) and use a 28-mm, a 50-mm, and a 80–200 zoom lens. Don't forget extra batteries. (Much more on camera and photography details in Chapter Ten.)

Credentials

Anything you have in print that corroborates that you are a writer, such as clips with your byline. Always bring a letter of assignment, if you have one, just in case someone demands to know if you are truly on assignment. I usually cross out sections that refer to payment and expenses before I photocopy it and show it; that's no one else's business.

If you have published a book, bring it and/or reviews of it.

Samples of the publications for which you are, or intend to be, writing also help establish your affiliations.

A business card is handy as well, especially in foreign countries where the exchange of cards is standard practice. It's also nice to translate into their language on the blank side of the card.

Small Address/Phone Book

You never know when you're going to have to write to or contact—or simply would just love to hear the comforting voice of—a friend, relative, or colleague. The new credit-card-sized pocket calculator/address books are the mobile society's salvation; they beat trying to lug along your Rolodex.

Research

Take only the best or what is necessary of what you've collected from your preliminary research. Bring maps and other essentials. Condense the rest into your notebooks to refer to while away. Don't bring much, because at the other end of your travels, if you have been doing your job correctly, you will be bringing back much more of the same.

Additional Baggage

Because of the aforementioned, you will need extra room to bring back what inevitably becomes more than you imagined. We're not taking souvenirs here, but the materials you will pick here, there, and everywhere—from hotel lobbies, museums, giveaways, flyers, tourism office packets. The travel writer's nickname is "sticky fingers."

Bring an empty day pack that you will use on your daily travels. For the flight home turn it into a portable office. Some seasoned travelers bring twelve-inch by fifteen-inch mailing envelopes that they fill and mail home throughout their trip.

Clothing

Our transient culture has deemed knowing how to travel a presumed skill. For travel writers the task is complicated by the fact that business is pleasure and pleasure is business. Your wardrobe has to accommodate an assortment of occasions.

My fantasy is that I'll take nothing, or almost nothing, traveling so light I can fit it all under my plane seat. Along the way I will pick up colorful and characteristic cheap local clothing. The reality is that in the interest of economy of money and time, I take utilitarian apparel, comfortable, loose-fitting sturdy clothing, some of which hand-washes easily. Besides, very rarely have I worn that big black fur Turkish hat I picked up for such a deal in the bazaar in Istanbul. On the other hand, the lungee I brought back from India served me well for many years. And buying—more frequently bartering—in the market-place always becomes a revealing encounter with the culture.

Always bring light rain gear, a hat, and any of the following: hiking shoes, sneakers, rubber sandals, slippers, or moccasins. Well before your journey, break in the shoes you will do most of your walking in or they will break your spirit very shortly.

More Reading

More reading? Yes, more reading. The good stuff: novels that feed the sense of place. Literature that uses place as a backdrop or even as a frontdrop. The only place you could have gotten me to read James Michener's *Hawaii* was Hawaii, and I loved it. Only in India would *The Autobiography of a Yogi* have made all the sense in the world. In Trinidad I read Trinidad-born novelist V. S. Naipaul's *The Middle Passage* and *Finding the Centre* and other novels and plays by local authors. Reading literature from around the world and seeing the pages come to life outside your room is fascinating, each experience giving greater meaning to the other. Also take that dog-eared mystery novel that's been sitting at your bedside for months. All of it keeps words moving through the recesses of your mind, as verbal backdrop to your experience.

Things I Never Take but Often Wish I Had

A flashlight, a second bathing suit, an extra pair of glasses and sunglasses, an extra copy of my assignment or itinerary. And, for the truly compulsive traveler, prestamped (domestic trips only) preaddressed envelopes and postcards, scissors, carbon paper, and a complete portable office. All dispensable travel accessories but at times priceless.

You might call all the preceding pretrip planning. But I wouldn't. It's the beginning of the trip itself; this is when you begin to set your creative/analytical reporter's mind in motion. All of it prepares you for:

Being There

Believe it or not, now comes one of the most difficult aspects of the whole endeavor: having a good time. No kidding. Some travel writers get so caught up in the "biz" they forget to enjoy themselves, to savor the moments. Granted, it's not easy to slow down and smell the cappuccino in real life, and it can be equally difficult while moving, moving, moving. But its benefits will be reflected in your prose, whether you intend it to or not.

Being there allows you to collect the juices in which you will marinate when you are at home writing. Hang out at that sunny bar, or in some shady plaza. Suck up ambience, let the mind drift. Revel. Have a great time. The problem with *really being there* is that you can get so comfortable that you decide the intelligent lifestyle alternative would be to unpack your bags and become a porch-sitting idiot somewhere like in Pokhara, Nepal. The consummate fool on the hill.

Setting Up Base Camp

Upon arriving at your destination, set up a temporary "office." Stack up your research, organize your maps. Have your phone book at hand. Review your itinerary. You may have to make several phone calls to inquire about reservations, reconfirm interviews, or double-check on museum or business hours. While you wait for the return calls, or the phone lines to be open, spend the time getting familiar with your portable office. I often end up spending the first several hours at my destination in my hotel room, my base camp, perhaps scribbling some first impressions and notes to myself. This all helps make sure there's a writer on the job here. The advantage of having a phone number where someone can reach you is important on the road, when you sometimes have only several days to make a connection. (The penny-wise travel writer should consider using the pay phone down the hall or in the lobby, since calls made from hotel rooms are convenient but exorbitant.)

Venturing Out

After the marathon phone session, get oriented. Drop your bags and take to the streets. Get to know the immediate vicinity and figure out the geography of the region as quickly as possible. Establishing place is just as important to the person as it will be to the prose.

Getting Around

Walk as much as possible; it's the best way to personally take the pulse of any city or country. The slow pace of bicycling also provides that experience, enforcing a tight geographic radius, and a tight editorial frame of reference. When taking taxis, buses, and planes, study faces and cultural quirks.

Get Lost!

Look at a map in the morning, put it in your back pocket, and with camera and notebook (plus hat and sweater or windbreaker) take off for the day and get lost—literally. With luck, you'll find hidden alleys and off-the-beaten-path museums. From such serendipitous encounters will entertaining prose emerge.

To Hire a Guide or Not?

A well-versed guide is worth the investment. To be really indulgent hire a private guide—it will probably be expensive—but then you can drill him with question after question and take him wherever you want to go. And you can write it off with other legitimate research expenses.

The Art of Interviewing

The French have a saying: "Who loses his language loses his faith." Seneca said: "Speech is the index of the mind." People are the key to any culture. And the key to people is their language. If you don't already have one, develop—beg, steal or borrow—an "ear for language." Speaking even a hundred words of a local language or dialect tunes you in to the people and their culture in a way nothing else can, not to mention the fact that it makes talking with local people, which you should do as often as possible, easier.

Being a travel writer "on assignment" gives you journalistic license to walk up to an interesting looking person and— charmingly, of course—ask all kinds of questions you're dying to ask anyway. And even some you weren't dying to ask.

Steinbeck already provided the secret of a good interviewer: "Listen . . ." Initiate conversations with all sorts of people. Prepare a series of questions beforehand. Is there some local custom you've noticed but would like to know more about? Are there any especially great things to do and see, unknown hikes or romantic restaurants? Is there some great folk lore known only to locals?

Get specific when interviewing people. People tend to talk in vague references. Get them to tell you what year *exactly*, what beach path *exactly*. And even how to spell it. All these questions should not allow your interviewee to digress, another common conversational habit. "And then what happened?" frequently gets people back on track. Or repeat the last thing they said of interest to you. The nuts-and-bolts information you cull from these questions helps produce prose that is, in fact, informative.

When interviewing, it's appropriate to introduce yourself as the writer of an article so that people know they may be quoted. If you say, "Mind if I ask you a couple of questions for this article I'm writing?" and they respond in the affirmative, you can assume they understand they may be quoted. The conversation is "on the record" unless they say otherwise. You do not need a signed release from them—similar to photographers' model releases—to mention them in your resulting article.

Writing on the Road

Some writers can sit down after a day on the streets and put a thousand words on paper. Some can't. Some suggest that getting it all down while it's fresh produces fresher copy. Others argue that time and distance give the writer a clearer picture of what was important and, like an aged wine, result in more profound insights. Hemingway said, "Never write about a place until you're away from it, because it gives you perspective. Immediately after you've seen something you can give a photographic description of it and make it accurate. That's good practice, but it isn't creative writing."

I suggest taking copious notes, at times letting the notes expand into paragraphs that attempt to capture a thought or a feeling, a look, taste, or smell. Save these notes and sketchy paragraphs; add them to your first draft material. There may be lines you can salvage to include in your piece, but for the most part they will serve as additional backdrop. These are the field notes to which you can refer, your firsthand observational data. Never, never let the fact that you are unable to write about a place while on the road—or that you can't imagine how you're going to write the piece when you get home—deter you from continuing researching the story and enjoying the trip. That would be self-defeating and pointless.

Some writers on the road enjoy writing (or feel obliged to write) letters. The epistolary form is a grand old literary tradition that the travel writer can take advantage of. Write letters—evocative, detailed, informational, introspective letters—to friends at home. In a P.S., ask them to save the letters and return them to you when you get back from your travels. This may seem narcissistic at first, but some great gems can be culled from such writing.

The same holds true for diary keepers, who may record extensive travel notes whether they plan to write about the trip for publication or not. Personally, though I have kept travel journals, I must admit I have never seen one word in them worth reprinting for anyone else's eyes. Nonetheless, those personal scribblings were early attempts at putting all my experiences into words. And worth the effort.

CHAPTER 7

Financial Factors: What Price Travel Writing?

Can We Talk?

To be sure, travel writing is one (legal) way to afford the leisure travel life you couldn't afford otherwise. But not unlike the rest of real life, there's no such thing as an entirely free lunch. There may be a considerable outlay of funds prior to earning anything. Like any start-up business or cottage industry, there may be a spell where the cash flow is horrendous, meaning cash will flow in a direction away from your wallet.

As you already know, traveling in any class is costly and, though the yen, mark, and dollar may fluctuate, we can rest assured that travel will get costlier. Most of the time you will have to front the money to finance a trip, even if a magazine pays for your expenses upon your return. If you sell a story afterward, the check and the reimbursement for your expenses may not be forthcoming until several months later. If, in the final analysis, you sum up what you made, what you spent, and how much time it all took (don't even think about all those hours you spent researching and writing a proposal, hours that no one pays you for), you may decide there are more lucrative career paths.

Let's be honest: This is a labor of love more than of money. Just breaking even in this business, however, makes you a winner: If you earn enough money to cover your travel expenses, you gained a free trip and a byline to boot—though, as my father would note, the latter and a token will get you a ride on the subway. Then again, no amount of money compensates for the personal satisfaction you get from seeing your name above a published article.

"Making it" as a travel writer depends on what your goals are. How serious do you want to get? Do you want to sell a travel story every couple of years? Or be a weekend or moonlighting freelance? Half-time while driving a cab? Or full-time? Do you want your earnings from travel writing to augment your other income? Or do you intend travel writing to be an opportunity for a more creative personal expression that is not available in your nine-to-five job?

My own goals overlapped a bit of all of the above. I began writing travel articles to supplement my income as a full-time freelance writer/lecturer/teacher. I never intended to write solely travel articles; that might be financial suicide. It would also induce stylistic myopia to write only in that genre. But I planned to write travel pieces every couple of months as a respite from my other work and to allow enough time to recuperate from one trip and plan for the next.

Newspaper travel sections pay the least of all markets—from as low as $25 and $35 to as high as $250 (*The New York Times*). The average is between $75 and $150, with the highest rates going to articles appearing on the first page of the section. The fees magazines pay for stories vary, depending on the length of the story, the caliber of the writer, and the quality of the magazine. On the low end you might garner $200 to $400 for 2,000-plus words. At the high end expect close to $1,500 or more (*National Geographic* still pays top fees of $5,000 and up). In the middle the fees range from $600 to $1,200.

What do you need to break into this line of work? When I started as a freelance writer in 1975 I had four things going for me—and none of them has talent. I had a wife who held a good job, I was collecting a monthly severance check from a previous employer, I had a part-time job teaching, and I had $10,000 in a bank, a considerable sum at the time. I also had a lot of chutzpah, a skill they do not teach in school but which can be developed.

Nuts and Bolts

First of all, I hope you kept the receipt for the purchase of this book: It's deductible. Keep receipts for everything short of breathing. Keeping receipts is the real sign of a seasoned travel writer.

In order to approach this business in a businesslike fashion—and therefore as a business deduction—you must document what it cost to write your article. So keep a daily log noting what you spent in pursuit of your story. It is important for you to know what your operating expenses are, but it is *essential* to those folks downtown at the federal building.

At the research stage, keep receipts for maps, books, photocopying, postage, tapes used for interviews, and telephone calls. If you take a bus to the local library, keep the bus receipt. A magazine may think you El Cheapo for submitting a receipt for that petty sum, which always strikes me as ironic when you see how much they spend on you for lunch at the publication's expense. Charging magazines for pens or notebooks, however, *is* going a little too far. Keep the receipts for your own records, though.

On the road keep receipts for expenses directly related to the story. If you were going to London for two weeks and planned on spending some of the time researching a story about London pubs, collect receipts for transportation to and from pubs, and for drinking and eating at the pubs. If you spent five days of fifteen working on the story, you may be able to deduct roughly one third of all your expenses.

If you were doing a general story on London and spent every day or part of every day working on the story, deduct the entirety of your expenses.

Keep stubs for entrance fees to museums, parks, theaters, or other entertainments related to your research.

Equipment purchased specifically for use on the trip is deductible. If you plan other uses for it after you've finished the assignment, you probably cannot deduct it. My accountant once thought about deducting a ten-speed bicycle I bought to write about biking on Martha's Vineyard one summer—a ten-speed I still owned fourteen years later. Wisely my accountant thought twice.

There may also be some expenses incurred once you return home, perhaps for a phone call back to someone you befriended who was following up on some information for you, or for another book that you may need for more background.

Who Pays Expenses and How Much?

If you have worked out an agreement with a publication that assigned you to do a travel story, it will stipulate your approximate expense limit. There are no rules as to exactly how much you'll get in expenses. Naturally, the better-paying and higher-quality publications pay more. One upscale magazine said it would pay as much in expenses as it paid for the story fee, which at the time was $600. That is rare. Rarer still is *National Geographic*, which several years ago advanced me $4,000 in two installments for a story they paid $3,000 for (it's rare to get a magazine to advance expenses). Most will say they cover "reasonable expenses," which of course begs questions because what is reasonable to one person may be unreasonable to another. Nonetheless, honor your expense limit. In fact, go under it if you really want to ingratiate yourself to an editor. Sometimes I absorb expenses out of my own pocket to stay on the good side of an editor who, after all, has to justify your expenses to someone else. In return, I hope editors will look forward to assigning me another story and possibly even loosening the purse strings a bit.

It is entirely appropriate and advisable to ascertain or reconfirm your expense agreement if an editor does not stipulate anything about it in the letter of assignment. Most freelances wimp out here. They figure they were lucky enough to get the assignment—why press their luck and appear ungrateful by asking for additional funding? But, in fact, editors will respect you all the more for your professionalism if you ask. You can suggest that you anticipate spending whatever amount and ask if the magazine would be able to pick up some or all of those expenses. You could also suggest the magazine pay for a specific part of the expenses, like hotels or car rentals.

A typical bill for expenses, on your stationery, would look like this:

Dear————:
   Please pay me, as agreed, for the following expenses incurred while researching the story on Israel for your magazine. The receipts are enclosed.

Telephone	$50.75
Taxi	35.00
Hotels	250.00
Books, Maps	20.00
Car Rental	115.25
Museum Fees	10.50
TOTAL	$481.50

  Sincerely,

  Perry Garfinkel

Claiming Expenses When Filing Income Tax Returns

The Tax Reform Act of 1986 added insult to injury in the struggling writer's life, throwing some curves that make you wonder if the IRS harbors a bias against freelance writers, all of whom it considers subversives—especially in view of the new twist that you cannot deduct the expense for something that did not earn you money in that same year.

But this fact remains true: In order to deduct travel expenses for a story, whether you were assigned to write it or wrote it speculatively, you have to prove that you had the intent to write about it *before you went.* How you prove it is by keeping records of expenses, and copies of dated query letters to editors, as well as copies of their responses, in the period before you traveled. Then, even if you have not gotten an assignment and take the trip anyway, you can prove that it was your "intent" to write about it. The final proof of your intent is to write the piece when you return and send it out on spec to publications, keeping a dated copy of the manuscript and the dated cover letter to editors (or a log of who you sent it to and when), as well as rejection letters.

How long can you deduct travel expenses without selling a story? Good question, though a better question would be how long *should* you remain in the red without selling a story? There are different views among accountants as to how long you can show losses before you start turning a profit. The average is a couple of years, which is fine, because if you're not showing some profit by then, perhaps you ought to be considering a different field altogether.

I am not nor have I ever been suspected of being a certified public accountant. Which is to say: Consult your accountant in regard to all this.

Who Else Can Help:
How to Arrange Complimentary Airfare,
Hotel, Wheels, Meals, and Masseuse

I discovered all this innocently enough. I had called the Mexican embassy in San Francisco looking for information about Mazatlán. They referred me to a public relations firm in Los Angeles that represented the government's tourism branch. Among other questions, I asked whether there was someone I might talk to about arranging complimentary airfare and hotel accommodations.

"Us," she said matter-of-factly.

A light bulb went on. What I came to realize was that every country that has a tourism development office—or a ministry of tourism or any government branch promoting tourism—also quite probably retains a public relations firm trying to get media coverage for its client. These P.R. firms not only produce the press packets and releases for travel writers, but they also set up various complimentary travel arrangements for travel writers. Governments, as well as hotels, airlines, and other privately owned tourism concerns, allot certain amounts of money in their budgets just for this purpose.

For example, here are the travel promotion budgets for the top ten American states for fiscal 1987: Illinois, $15.5 million; New York, $14.8 million; Pennsylvania, $11.9 million; Michigan, $11.8 million; Tennessee, $10.8 million; Florida, $10.8 million; Massachusetts, $9.4 million; Hawaii, $8.5 million; New Jersey, $8.1 million; and California, $7.8 million.

These firms arrange press junkets on which they invite travel writers who are known to contribute regularly to good "outlets" (their word for newspapers and magazines), even if those writers do not already have an assignment. Who they invite is definitely a subjective affair. Getting on that list of favored writers involves writing about their client in high-circulation publications; it's that simple. Once you do get on such a list, you will be invited from time to time on all-expense-paid trips of varying lengths to destinations of varying degrees of exotica.

If you are not yet a favored writer but are planning a trip for which you have a letter of assignment from a reputable publication, and do not want to or cannot travel with a group at the time the press junket is planned, then you can approach the P.R. people on your own, asking them to help arrange complimentary hotel rooms, plane tickets, and whatever else you need on an individual basis. So, for instance, you could call a Hilton International hotel anywhere in the world or its corporate office in New York and talk to the public relations representative. Or you could call, for example, Pan Am's public relations or promotion director, headquartered in New York.

You could also call the local office of an airline and ask for a regional sales manager, who could assist you or direct you to the appropriate person.

The key, of course, is the letter of assignment, which P.R. firms or hotels will ask to see, With it, many doors open. But before that is the "understanding."

As I mentioned earlier, there's no such thing as a free lunch. The "understanding" is that in return for accommodating you, you will accommodate them by supplying laudatory prose about their client to the reading public.

Now, this causes ethical dilemmas for righteous and self-righteous journalists who like to remind anyone who will listen that they can't be bought. If we accept a freebie, their reasoning goes, we will feel obligated to write something nice about their hotel, airline, etc., whether we have something nice to say or not. It will force writers to mention a facility at the expense of good writing and good journalism. Philip Sousa, travel editor of the *San Diego Union*, cited the obviously subsidized story that began, "As my Pan Am flight descended over Port-of-Spain, the Trinidad Hilton stood out like a shining gem . . ."

In order to maintain journalistic objectivity, the reasoning continues, travel writers should not accept so-called sponsored trips. This sort of reasoning prohibits newspapers like *Newsday* and *The New York Times* from buying stories from writers who are in the habit of accepting freebies.

On the other hand, from the travel writer's point of view, considering the high cost of travel, it would be nearly impossible to see and do as much as is necessary to write well about a destination without some sort of financial assistance. What to do? As a professional journalist who cares about maintaining journalistic integrity, I have accepted assistance while reserving the right to say anything I want—or nothing at all—about a hotel, airline, restaurant or country.

I rationalize my policy—and don't lose sleep wrestling with my guilt—in this way: The travel industry operates on the domino principle. Gain for one is gain for all. Promotion and publicity for one hotel promote the whole region, and any facility doing its own advertising and other marketing will capitalize on the overflow of interest that will accrue from the published story. If the Flea-Bag Hotel in Mazatlán put me up for free, but I choose to recommend the Four-Star Hotel down the road, the Flea-Bag will eventually benefit when the overbooked Four-Star turns guests away. In addition, most hotels are in conspiracy with the local tourism promotion interests and realize that the goal is to promote the region first. Their promotion budgets often cover the cost of the free room, which for them is usually a drop in the bucket.

Travel and tourism are big business. In some states and countries they are among the biggest. It behooves the industry to support the best writers who will produce the best stories.

As widely published travel writer/photographer Lee Foster (read more about him in Chapter Nine) puts it:

"The consumer is best served by a professional travel writer who, in order to report on the best travel opportunities, must have a chance to experience as much as possible. I've got to take ten cruises to know who's offering what and where to get the best buys. Since travel and tourism is one of the biggest industries in most state and countries—it's the third-largest industry in California—the industry should help develop the best travel writing possible.

"In terms of 'being bought' I think that isn't an issue among those who consider themselves professional. The only responsibility of a professional travel writer is to present to the reader what he or she has seen and experienced, and to let the chips fall where they may. A travel writer who is in it for the long haul must see his or her research as cumulative. If I accept a free trip to visit a dude ranch in Montana, I may not write about it immediately, but three years later, when I am writing a story about things to do in Montana, then I will pull my file on that dude ranch and mention it. People in the tourism industry who help writers should understand that."

CHAPTER 8

Now That You're Published: The Follow-Through and Other Strategies for Getting More Work

Court Editors

After publishing, self-promotion is what the travel writer who wants to keep writing should do.

Promote yourself to the editor who just published you; immediately hit him with some more ideas. Strike while your name is still hot. Make sure your letterhead has your name prominently displayed in bold fashion-forward colors. Even if those ideas don't sell, presenting them helps maintain an ongoing relationship. Keeping your name in the editor's mind is the object.

Try calling to "chat about" a story idea before you put it in writing. (If you really want to test the waters of your status, try calling collect.) If you get a curt response, back off and excuse yourself quickly. You never can tell when an editor is on a deadline. Sometimes, however, especially if your previous story was well received, a brief conversation could turn into strong encouragement, if not a tentative assignment, which is what you're looking for. It could result in the editor suggesting an alternative angle, or you could end up getting assigned to a story that has been kicking around in the editor's head and is in need of a writer.

Keep editors abreast of what you're up to lately. Send them copies of stories you published elsewhere. Let them know your upcoming travel plans and interests. Drop them a postcard from some enticing locale. "Having a wonderful time. Wish you were here . . ." All of it helps sell you to editors as a widely published and well-traveled author.

Though it may be difficult, at all times remember that editors are people too. It is entirely possible to break through the professional writer–editor relationship and become friends. Nurture friendly but professional relationships with editors in the same manner that a good salesman develops more than business liaisons with accounts. Send a birthday card. Ask about family. Inquire about travel and vacation plans. Suggest a social get-. together the next time you're in town. Take an editor to a play or movie he's expressed interest in. It's a good investment— and tax deductible.

This is a people-to-people business. The more personable you are, the more enjoyable you are to talk with and work with, the more inclined editors will be to think kindly of you, which is a nice feeling regardless of how you write.

Publishing is a volatile industry. Magazines fold. Heads roll. Staff changes are fast and furious. It's like musical chairs. When the music stops, an editor you knew from X magazine is now an editor at Y newspaper. And since it is a people-to-people business, most loyalties are to people, not publications. So when your friend the editor resurfaces somewhere else, call him. You may be in a position to get assignments and break into a new market.

Your Expanding Worldwide Fan Club

Stay in touch with people you meet on the road. A travel writer is only as good as his worldwide contacts. Besides knowing you have friends in remote places around the global community, those people out there whom you met—who helped you, whom you helped—are a growing network of friends who may be sources for ideas and information in the future. They are your scouts and stringers, for which you reimburse them with the grand opportunity of vicariously being part of the exotic life of an international travel writer (that's you). You may also promise to take them to dinner when you score an assignment that sends you back to their corner of the world—this time on some magazine's expense account. Eventually your bulging address book of international pen pals can become your worldwide mailing list, to whom you can market whatever it is you're selling.

To those people around the world who helped you, the nicest thing you could send them is a copy of the article they helped you publish—that and an open invitation to camp out in your living room the next time they visit your area.

Grease the Way for Your Next Sponsored Accommodation

A copy of the published article is also what will ingratiate you to those people who provided complimentary airfare, hotel room, car, food or anything else. Most of them subscribe to clipping services, so they will get a copy eventually, but they may not—and the personal connection is what you want to nurture anyway. Send copies or tear sheets, with a cover letter thanking them for helping make the story possible. If you truly did mention the facility and the editor cut the mention, send your original manuscript with the copy of the published piece. Also, promote yourself further by sending them something else you've published recently and reminding them of your interest in leads for other stories.

Remarketing, Spinning off, Reprinting, Reselling, Rewriting, and Other Ways to Make Your Trip Keep Paying for Itself

Some say the only way to make it financially as a travel writer is by remarketing your stories—selling the same story to different newspapers and magazine for reprint rates, or by revising parts of the story to "spin it off" in a slightly different direction, with a slightly different angle. This is often accomplished by refocusing the beginning paragraphs of the story, then weaving into the main body of your story, which remains almost unchanged except for some shifting of paragraphs or tightening of transitions. Here are two versions of the same story, the first written for a magazine, the second for newspapers:

The Transformation of Loreto

The Baja village destined to become Mexico's newest resort

by Perry Garfinkel

On the streets of Loreto, it's hot, dry, and dusty—as one would expect in any town on the Baja. Not even the breeze from the Sea of Cortés, shimmering only several hundred feet away, negates the heat.

But appearances deceive. The sleepy facade of this mild-mannered Mexican town, on the east coast of the Baja California peninsula stretching 700 miles south of San Diego, conceals a rich past, a vibrant present, and a very promising future.

Known only to fishermen for years, Loreto, the oldest permanent settlement in all the Californias, is now being called the next Cancún or Ixtapa. Following elaborate computer analyses, Fonatur, the Mexican government's tourism development project, selected the village as its newest resort region. Plans call for the creation of a tourist zone along the bay of Nopoló, about four miles south of Loreto, and an upgrading of facilities in Loreto itself. Within two years, the town's population is expected to increase from 6,000 to 16,000, and the number of annual visitors should increase from 50,000 to half a million by 1990.

Plot Development

Loreto is presently in what is called Phase I, when improvements on basic facilities such as water and electricity take place. A pattern of paved streets lined with telephone poles and utility wires already stretches out from Loreto's center, transforming it into a ghostly town of the future waiting to be subdivided and developed.

There are now about 500 hotel rooms in the area, in half a dozen hotels including the luxurious 250-room *El Presidente Hotel* on the bay of Nopoló. But within two years there will be more than 1,000; by 1988 that figure will double. (Club Med has already expressed interest in building the next hotel on the bay.)

This winter a marina sporting 100 boat slips will be completed at nearby Puerto Escondido, one of the best natural hurricane havens in the Sea of Cortés. Visitors can already charter simple fishing skiffs throughout the area, but this season a greater variety of nautical recreational equipment— Windsurfers, sailboats, cabin cruisers, and scuba gear—will be available. In the town itself, a 300-seat restaurant–conference center will open this winter, and the concrete seaside walkway, or *malecón*, as well as the town plaza, will be spiffed up. At Nopoló, an equestrian center, an eighteen-hole golf course, a sports center, plus villas, condos, and hotels are in the blueprint stage.

It's quite an ambitious vision, especially in view of a supporting economy that seems as stable as a Mexican jumping bean. But even if the project can't be completed in such grand fashion, current travel bargains in Mexico—and the attractions of Loreto itself—should guarantee a large number of visitors. The town has easy access to the ten-year-old Transpeninsular Mexico Highway 1, as well as a landing strip that has recently been expanded to accommodate jets; an excellent climate; a good water supply; and a fascinating history.

Mission Accomplished

The Spanish explorer Juan Maria Salvatierra settled Loreto in 1697. Loreto remained capital of the Californias for 70 years and of Baja until 1828. The first mission in the Californias was established there in 1720, dedicated to the virgin Nuestra Señora de Loreto. It was from this mission at the foot of the jagged Sierra de la Giganta mountain range that Father Junípero Serra set out on foot in 1769 to establish a chain of missions extending some 1,500 miles north into what is now Sonoma, California.

San Javier, the second oldest mission and one of the best preserved, is a two-hour drive from Loreto through 21 miles of classically barren but beautiful Baja desert into the heart of the Sierra. The tough trek ends in the tiny village of San Javier, where the mission, built from volcanic rock, rises up at the end of a dusty boulevard 50 feet high to the bell tower.

The history of old Loreto has been preserved at the Mission Museum in town, on Salvatierra Road (open daily except Mondays). A ten-year restoration by the National Institute of Anthropology and History has resulted in surprisingly sophisticated displays of photos, maps, clothing, crafts, tools, weapons, and religious artifacts.

Looking at Loreto today it's hard to believe that it was once a thriving commercial center. In 1829 a devastating hurricane virtually destroyed the original town, and the one built in its place was small and leisurely—*tranquilo,* as the Mexicans say.

Loreto's major attraction has always been its waters, some of the richest fishing areas in all of Mexico. Four hundred species populate the Cortés—among them yellowtail, yellowfin tuna, dolphin, marlin, sailfish, grouper, sea bass, papagallo, and red snapper. The catch is plentiful year-round, but from March to July the waters are filled with the greatest variety.

A half-hour out to sea lies Isla Coronado, abandoned by all but sea lions, where one can lie on a white-sand beach reminiscent of a Greek island's. Desert lovers may prefer Primer Agua, an oasis a scant four miles in from the highway. The El Presidente shuttles its guests there to enjoy picnics under the palms. The local specialty is chocolate-colored clams, barbecued in coals under tumbleweed, then stuffed into tortillas and topped with a spicy mustard sauce.

Eventually, a string of hotels will wind around the beach at Nopoló. But for now El Presidente has the sand all to itself. The two-year-old hotel, plush by Baja standards, can serve as a destination in itself or a night's relief from highway driving or el cheapo hotels. Rooms are $40 a night, double occupancy (Boulevard Misión de Loreto: Loreto; telephone 30700). Other hotels in Loreto include the *Hotel Oasis* (Box 17; Loreto; telephone 30112) and the *Hotel Misión de Loreto* (Box 49; Loreto; telephone 30048, in the United States 916-925-6766).

The restaurant at the Hotel Misión de Loreto, facing the sea, is the best in town. Guests may sit outside or inside for shrimp and vegetables on a skewer or three kinds of lobster dishes. On Saturday nights the restaurant holds a Mexican fiesta, with buffet tables full of local foods and the air full of mariachi music. On such occasions one doesn't need a computer to know that Loreto is alive and well—and heading for a future to rival its past.   ∎

"Old Loreto's Next Mission: To Become the Newest Mexican Resort"

By Perry Garfinkel

LORETO, Baja California, Mexico—They're calling this the next Cancun.

After a computer analysis, the Mexican government has picked this small village 700 miles south of San Diego on the Sea of Cortez as its next major tourist resort region.

By 1985 this town of 4,000 residents will exceed 16,000. The 500 hotel rooms that exist now will mushroom to 3,000. Over half a million annual visitors are projected by 1988.

So what does this area have going for it that has Fonatur, the Mexican tourism development branch, dumping millions of investment dollars into its shores? Nothing—besides five miles of sand beach, fascinating history, fabulous fishing and near-perfect climate. Also, the ever pragmatic computer notes, good water supply, easy access to the 1,000-mile transpeninsular Mexico Hwy. 1 and a second landing strip recently expanded for jets.

Of course, there is a qualified *if* to all this, depending on the stability of the Mexican government and its ability to fund the ambitious project.

With the peso lately as stable as a jumping bean, it's anybody's guess as to whether the venture will be realized in the grandiose style envisioned—or at all.

BUT FOR THE itinerant Baja traveler who can't wait for the new marina, equestrian center, 18-hole golf course, 300-seat restaurant/entertainment center and the rows of villas, condos and hotels, Loreto's lure is as strong today as it must have been in 1697 when Spanish explorers made it the first permanent settlement in all of the Californias.

Here at the foot of the imposing red and green hued Sierra de la Giganta range, the first mission in the Californias was completed in 1752 and dedicated to the virgin Nuestra Sonora de Loreto. From here Father Juniper Serra set foot in 1769 to establish a chain of missions that eventually extended some 1,500 miles north.

Today, after a 10-year restoration by the National Institute of Anthropology and History, you can see old Loreto in period clothing, crafts, tools, weapons and religious artifacts at the mission museum on Salvatierra Road [open daily except Monday, no charge].

The second oldest mission is San Javier, said to be one of the best preserved. From Loreto, the grueling but beautiful 22-mile two-hour drive into the heart of the Sierra reveals the tiny oasis-green village where about 70 families live pretty much the way their ancestors did when the mission was built 225 years ago. The edifice, constructed with indigenous volcanic rock, is the centerpiece of town, soaring 50 feet to the bell tower. The Moorish architecture and elaborate stonework have withstood the elements remarkably well.

LOOKING AT Loreto today, it is hard to believe it was once the capital of Baja California and a thriving commercial center for the entire peninsula. A devastating hurricane in 1829 destroyed that town. The one rebuilt in its place was small and leisurely—or *tranquilo,* as the Mexicans say. It looks now like many of the dusty rural towns that dot the length of Baja.

Some say you can find excellent local white cheese [*queso*

Chihuahua] but, as it has been since its beginnings, the major attraction of Loreto can be found off its shores—some of the fish-richest waters on either side of the Baja peninsula. Four hundred species populate the waters of the Cortez—yellowtail, grouper, tarpon, dorado, tuna, sea bass, pompano, rooster, sierra rande and more—and for reasons Loreto locals attribute to luck and providence the catch is plentiful year-round. Seasonal game fishing is equally rewarding. One local hotel recorded 3,000 striped marlin caught in one season.

Alfredo Ramirez, a taciturn but warm-hearted former resident of Sacramento, moved here 12 years ago and now runs the best fishing boat fleet from the local pier [P.O. Box 39, Loreto, Baja California Sur, Mexico; telephone 30165]. Ramirez charges $70 for a day-long trip and he takes pity on neo- and non-anglers by dropping them off for a secluded beach picnic on uninhabited [except for the sea lions] Coronado Island, a half-hour from Loreto. When you come back, he'll smoke your catch for 80 cents a pound.

AS FOR THE Loreto of the future, it can be seen under a plastic bubble—in an architect's scale model—at Fonatur's regional office five miles south of town. If all goes as scheduled, there will be paved streets, a boardwalk, a facelifting to the town plaza, a sports arena and more. Developers see the urban center and its historical significance as important tourism attractions, but the real magnet of this area is the five-mile half-moon beach smiling out on the Bay of Nopolo and Coronado and Carmen Islands.

Eventually there will be a half-dozen luxury hotels, as well as condominiums and villas, necklacing this beach. For now the government's own El Presidente has the white sand spread all to itself. A plush 250-room hotel with a very good French restaurant and a very good disco [considering the local competition—none], the 2-year-old El Presidente is either a destination in itself or a night's relief from highway driving, sandy sleeping bags or el cheapo hotels. Rooms are $40 a night for a double [Boulevard Mision de Loreto, Loreto; telephone 30700].

THERE ARE two good hotels facing the sea in downtown Loreto that evoke a sense of Loreto's more recent past. The Hotel Oasis [P.O. Box 17, Loreto; telephone 30112] has large rooms with modern furnishings and a restaurant overlooking the beach. Double rooms are $40, including three meals a day. Across the road is the Hotel Misión de Loreto [P.O. Box 49, Loreto; telephone 30048; U.S. phone, 916-925-6766]. High ceilings and hand-painted tiling are featured in the rooms. Rates are $20 for a single or double; add $10.50 per person for three meals. The newest hotel in Loreto is the government-run Las Pintas, a 20-room, quieter and less luxurious version of the El Presidente. Rooms are spacious, with red tile floors, intricate woodwork and antique wood furniture. The hotel also has a pool and a restaurant. Rooms are about $15–$17 a night for double occupancy.

Until the completion of the Baja Highway, only private boats and planes made it to Loreto. Seven years ago Air Cortez be-gan flying there from Ontario and San Diego, with its commercial fleet of Fairchild 27s and Twin Beech eight-seat prop planes. Round-trip air fare from Ontario is $260; from San Diego, $230. Both stop en route in Guaymas, Mexico. The airline also offers a package including air fare and five days/four nights at either the El Presidente [$350] or the Mision de Loreto [$300). Air Cortez's toll-free number in California is 800-221-1203; outside it's 800-221-1197.

AeroMexico [800-252-0361] also now flies round trip from Los Angeles to Loreto for $200, and will arrange connecting flights from San Francisco on PSA, TWA and United.

Reprint Rates

For reprint rates, expect half to two thirds of the original fee. There are no cut-and-dried rules on how much you can get, or more precisely how much an editor will choose to offer. But there ought to be a standardized rate system. Why not? TV and screen writers' fees are established by the Writer's Guild, photographers' fees are established by the American Society of Magazine Photographers. Let us pray for strength in the young National Writers Union or similar institutions.

Except when a contract stipulates otherwise, you are usually selling a publication the rights for one-time use. Be wary of selling all rights to anything. First North American rights means, quite literally, that it hasn't appeared previously in North

America. As soon as it appears, however, you are free to resell it. Read up more on copyright laws or ask an expert for more details. What you need to know here is that writers don't make much from selling their work and should be allowed to use every opportunity they can seize to sell it.

Send the manuscript of a story you are offering for resale, not a clip or photocopy of the piece as it appeared in another publication. Editors don't like to see what they are about to publish already in print.

For your efforts (which may entail only reprinting your story from a computer or making clean, clear photocopies, plus the time invested in putting the manuscript, cover letter, and other samples of your work in an envelope, addressing it, and mailing it) and for your cost (the postage, the envelope, the paper; probably about a dollar per publication), you may add as little as twenty-five dollars to your coffers, or you may make as much as several thousand dollars if you resell the piece a dozen times to high-paying markets. Plus you get that immeasurable commodity: exposure. Your name is read by readers, writers, and editors. This will not pay the rent, but it increases your worth over time. People become familiar with you or your byline. Your fees go up as you get more widely published.

There is another plus: Your words, experiences, thoughts, and feelings are related to another person and perhaps that person is moved in some way. There is no way to put a price tag on that either. But it's why we keep writing.

CHAPTER 9

Future Tense: Travel Writing Meets the Computer Age

I have seen the future of travel writing and it is ensconced in a two-by-nothing pine-panelled basement cubbyhole in Oakland, California. There, it is embodied in one Lee Foster, a tall, lean fellow with a touch of wildness in his eyes but an altogether feet-on-the-ground approach to the profession of travel writing.

Last year Foster's words and photographs were published in twenty-five magazines and twenty-eight newspapers. He is the author of several regional travel guides, as well as books on his other love, organic gardening.

He also holds the distinction of being the first travel writer to produce the first travel guide books available on computer disks. And he is the first to publish any kind of book in three modes—in print ($11.95), on floppy disk ($19.95), and on-line via CompuServe ($6 per hour), a computerized database service available by modem through the telephone.

If Marco Polo were alive today, he would be taking lessons from Lee Foster.

All this produces about thirty thousand to forty thousand dollars to support himself, his wife, and their three children. But, hey, he gets to travel.

A literature Ph.D. candidate at Stanford in the mid-sixties, Lee "saw an alternative" and decided to combine his interest in photography and writing with his insatiable wanderlust. What else was there to do but become a freelance travel writer? He also brought an entrepreneurial spirit and picked up a bit of computer savvy when he saw the writing on the wall—or, in this case, the pulsing cursor on the monitor. In the early eighties, he bought his first Osborne personal computer, now a relic.

His office is now aclutter with computer hardware. His main machine is an MS-DOS clone, with a hard disk that has a twenty-megabyte memory and 640K RAM. He has two printers: a Diablo, which produces letter quality only; and a Toshiba 321, a twenty-four-pin dot matrix printer with draft and near-letter-quality modes.

Except for his actual travels, and occasional trips to the kitchen, Lee never has to leave his claustrophobic "garret" to get his words and images to editors and readers around the world. It's all done through the miracle marriage of computer and telephone.

He "modems" his stories to a growing number of newspapers and magazines, some of whom will now work only with freelances who can telecommunicate their stories. A modem (which costs between $100 and $300) is a device that connects your computer to your telephone line and allows you to send and receive information from your computer to another computer/modem/telephone setup. In a matter of minutes you can send several thousand words from your computer to another computer by dialing the receiving phone number and entering the appropriate access codes. He can also bypass the endless-wait-in-the-post-office-line scene by "mailing" his manuscript electronically to a phone number at an MCI facility nearest the editorial offices of the publication for which he's writing. MCI then prints out the manuscript on paper (as "hard copy"), and on the same day drops it in the local mail stream. In effect, you get overnight mail service similar to Federal Express or Express Mail, except that FedEx and other overnight postal services cost from ten dollars to twenty dollars, plus often a trip to the nearest dispatching office. By using the MCI "paper mail" system, the cost is approximately one dollar per page, including the printout, postage, and handling.

On the road Lee is state-of-the-art as well. He recently retired his Toshiba T1100, a portable laptop personal computer that weighed nine pounds and cost two thousand dollars when he purchased it in 1987. Now he totes the six-pound T1000 (eight hundred to one thousand dollars), which is nine inches by nine inches and two inches deep, and can store the equivalent of 280 manuscript pages (700K) on a three-and-a-half-inch disk. When he gets home, he can download all his field notes into his main computer.

But that's only a glimpse of the Brave New Travel Writing World According to Lee Foster. What he is into now may change forever how we think of the genre. Or at least how we get access to it.

In 1984 Foster became the first to make travel articles he'd written available through CompuServe, the supermarket of databases that offers everything from the Dow Jones closing averages to the Grolier Academic Encyclopedia. His "West Coast Travel" provides articles about one hundred destinations in the West; travel questions and answers; special-interest travel; new trends in travel; and a new Silicon Valley Guide. His "Adventures in Travel" offers fifty write-ups about worldwide travel, with a new one added every two weeks.

Foster promises at the outset that all the write-ups are based on his personal travel research in the field. A typical article is about twenty-five hundred words long and, while lacking any great stylistic distinction, is comprehensive and informative (an

"If You Go" section ends each article). Foster patterns most articles similarly so you'll know what to expect: sections are subtitled "Flavor of the Place," "Getting There," "History of the Area," "Main Attractions," "Nearby Trips," And "For Further Information."

A subscriber pays CompuServe for the amount of time he is on-line, at the rate of $6 per hour. On an average, Foster reports, people spend about ten minutes per call. Of that, Foster collects ten percent. In a typical week, about four hundred people call; he estimates he earns about forty dollars a week from this venture.

The floppy disks, "Lee Foster's Travel Disks," cover thirteen western states and areas of Canada and Mexico. Other available categories are "Special Interest Travel" (including winter sports, cruise travel, recreational vehicle travel) and "Adventures in Travel" (such as "Germany's Romantic Ruins," "France's Burgundy Wine Country," and "Minnesota's Lake Country").

In all there are over 150 write-ups, and the list increases in direct proportion to Foster's travels. All 150 articles on disk are available for $150. Customized disks, in which the subscriber chooses stories from among the entire list, can be ordered as well ($19.95 for 10 write-ups).

Foster points out some of the advantages of travel guide books on disk:

They are compact, taking up a small portion of a shelf, especially compared to the space taken by books, magazines, and the mess of newspaper clippings that make corners of my office look like a condo complex for hamsters.

You can print out only sections that interest you. And you can take the printout with you to a destination. You can write on and destroy that printout because you can always make another.

The disks are interactive, meaning you can insert additional or updated information, or cynical asides to create a new editorial product. (Foster suggests: "You might want to copy a file to a blank disk, for example, and begin your own lifelong travel records from that area.")

For the futuristic-thinking travel writer, Foster's services provide not only instant access to background materials for your own writing but a model for how to make your work available in as many media modes as possible.

This information is presented in view of the fact that even as the ink dries on this page, computer technology will have transmogrified to such a degree that it may well be immaterial or at least irrelevant. As we speak, the present becomes the past and the future could look like this:

Winter. Massachusetts. 2001.

We are all on-line. Access to almost anything almost anywhere is possible by hitting a couple of keys at your fingertips. You dial up Lee Foster and a giant screen on the living room wall becomes undulating Pacific waters and black sand beaches on the southern shores of the Big Island of Hawaii. Hologrammed hummingbirds fly overhead, the scents of coconut and hibiscus are in the air. You are completely surrounded by a new environment, aware of every sense. Lee's voice-over welcomes you to a tour of underwater caves. You dive. Submersion. There and then is here and now.

CHAPTER 10

Travel Photography: A Picture Is Worth a Thousand Words and, Sometimes, a Thousand Dollars

It's humbling for a writer to admit, but here it is: good travel photographs can help sell even a mediocre travel manuscript. That's one reason to either learn how to shoot good pictures or find someone who does.

Editors, by necessity, must think in terms of "story packages"— that is, a combination of words and pictures ("art," as they sometimes call photographs or other illustrations). In most cases, every article must be accompanied by some sort of art. Despite what people who write words would like to think, print is a visual medium. Editors know that well-displayed dramatic photos might get you to read an average story.

Since editors will eventually have to find art somewhere to run with your story, you can save them time—and possibly make yourself extra money—if you can provide pictures as well. If you can't provide your own photos, editors often appreciate it when a writer can recommend a good photographer who would be interested in working with you.

As a result, because I was an average writer aspiring to be a good writer, and because I was a mediocre photographer with no aspirations of becoming a good photographer, and because I wanted to sell my travel stories, the first thing I did as a neophyte freelance was to hook up with a good professional freelance photographer—one with whom I also felt an affinity as a person and as a visualist, one I could learn from and, not coincidentally, one who also happened to have a lot of contacts with publications that he was willing to share with me.

The second thing I did was get a good camera and learn how to use it.

I suggest you do both if you want to sell your travel stories.

There are two reasons to take pictures on the road while researching a travel story. One is with an eye toward the markets. The other is with an eye toward your eye.

Whether you plan to try to sell your pictures or not, bring a camera on your travels and use it. Taking pictures makes you look more closely at your subject, and see more carefully in a variety of lights and lightings. In case you haven't noticed, the jargon of picture-taking is the same as the jargon of writing: in both, you "focus," "frame," "find an angle." In both you set a subject against a backdrop. In both you try to freeze a moment in time. In both you can make interesting juxtapositions. In both you can come in close on a specific, from which we can understand the general.

Cameras make you look, the most important sensory skill the travel writer can develop. However, if you "look" at the expense of "seeing"—that is, seeing the Big Picture—you may develop a kind of story blindness. Like the tourist who sees all his travel experiences only through the lens, you will miss seeing the Big Picture.

Another good reason to take photographs on the road is to have a visual record of your travels. Unlike the tourist's sentimental souvenirs, however, your photos are visual field notes that you will later surround yourself with when you are writing the story at home. Lay out the prints and slides and contact sheets and refer to them frequently while you are writing so that what the place looks like will come through in your words. They will help you bring there-and-then back to here-and-now as you write.

Once you decide to start taking better photographs, there are many photography books representing the full range of technicality. Buy as many as you want or need. I recommend *How to Get the Best Travel Photographs* by Fredrik D. Bodin, a yeoman freelance photographer who works and lectures widely. It is an easy-to-follow guide for someone whose primary focus is writing or for someone who simply wants better pictures from his or her travels; it succinctly presents the basics of what you'll need to know to get started. The following is excerpted from it.

How To Get the Best Travel Photographs

By Fredrik D. Bodin

The voyager with a camera is a special character in foreign countries. In many ways, the traveling photographer is unique in the sea of tourists. You are more sensitive and aware of the cultural environment. Your antennae are up; you're approachable. You are there to observe, to learn, and to enjoy. The camera is your visitor's badge. The camera links you more directly to the traveling experience. It is difficult, if not impossible, to separate yourself from your pictured subjects. When you're taking pictures, you've got a recognized license to loiter, fumble, gawk and chat with perfect strangers.

Travel Photographer's Checklist:

(Necessary)
Camera with sturdy strap.
50-mm or 55-mm normal lens.

24-mm or 35-mm wide-angle lens.
85-mm to 500-mm or zoom telephoto lens.
Filters (UV, polarizing).
Lens cleaning brush, tissue, fluid.
Fresh batteries.
Film (black and white and color).
Camera bag.

(Optional)
Close-up attachments.
Teleconverter.
Hand-held light meter.
Electronic flash.
Tripod.
Cable release.
Instant camera.

Framing

When you look through the viewfinder, imagine you're look-ing at the final picture. Move things around in the picture until they're to your liking. Like moving furniture, change the cam-era angle, arrange the subject, tidy up the background. The work you do before pressing the button is much more impor-tant than what happens after.

Get close. Many pictures fail simply because the photogra-pher was too far away from the subject. Get twice as close to the subject as you think you should. You paid for the whole piece of film, so you might as well fill it with the subject.

Don't always center. Always placing the subject dead center is an unconscious bad habit. A centered horizon line places emphasis on neither land nor sky. Use "the rule of thirds" to find alternatives to centering. Place the main subject in line with an imaginary vertical line a third of the way from the left-hand border.

Interesting angles. Pictures always taken at eye level can be tedious. Climb up high for a bird's-eye view. Get down low to make your subject look big. Look for natural frames and colorful objects to shoot through.

Simplify. Distracting backgrounds, irrelevant objects and clutter can ruin your pictures. Use your camera to make one clear statement at a time. A simple, direct photo is much stronger than a jumbled one.

Tips on Typical Travel Shooting

There are some tried and true situations that we will always want to take a picture of, cliche or not. And, in our beginner's naivete, we may even come up with some original images. Here are some tips for those situations.

Aquariums

Short of scuba diving, there is no better way to photograph live fish than to visit an aquarium. To get the best photograph, press your lens against a clean place on the glass to eliminate unwanted reflections. Take a light meter reading with the meter facing toward the bottom of the tank. Use this setting, and not one taken looking up toward the surface.

No filtration is needed for black-and-white film. Color film, however, will take on a blue cast when used under water. And the deeper the water, the bluer it gets. A CC30 red filter is a good general purpose filter that removes the blue cast under water. Below 30 feet, filtration is futile.

Flash produces vivid and sharp underwater pictures without filtration. If the aquarium allows it, use your portable flash, especially in deeper water. Press both the camera and the flash flush against the glass for shooting.

Cathedrals

Approach a cathedral exterior as if it were a landscape, using daylight film. Shoot from across the square or plaza, framing the entire building with the plaza in the foreground. Activity in the plaza, flying pigeons or robed monks, will enliven your exterior photos.

Stained glass, illuminated by the sun, is best photographed with daylight film. The large dark area surrounding the windows will mislead your light meter. To get a good exposure of the stained glass take a close-up reading and lock it in. If a close-up is not possible, take an exposure for the light level found outside. Next, take three more shots, each time opening up the lens by one stop (for example, from 1/125 at f/11 to f/8 to f/5.6 to f/4). This is called "bracketing" your exposures.

Large cathedrals often have candlelit alcoves. Use fast color film to compensate for the low level of existing light. Try to predetermine the exposure in an unoccupied alcove and lock it in. Now step back and, with a short telephoto, look for a worshiper lighting candles or in prayer. It may be necessary to steady your camera on a column or pew. Be discreet by not using flash, not closing in, and not taking too many photos.

Colors inside a cathedral will be a warm yellow-orange when shot on daylight film. I find such color adds to the warm feeling I want to create for this candlelight environment. For accurate color rendition, however, use tungsten-balanced color film with filtration.

Cityscapes

Professional travel photographers joke about shooting at dawn, napping all day and shooting again at sunset. At these times colors are their most exotic, shadows are defined, everything glows. Wait for this dramatic light—it's worth it.

Just before sunset, go to the highest observation point you dare to climb—a building or a nearby mountain. Bring a tripod (I view tripods with the same affection I do a clumsy old friend; they're a nuisance at times, but it's nice to have them when you need them). Most sane people will be on their way to dinner so you won't be crowded. If shooting through glass, position your lens flush up against it to eliminate inside reflections. (Draping a coat over your head and the camera will also help with reflections.) Lock in a meter reading of the ground below if you want detail to show there. For a rich sky at sunset, take a reading of the sky, but be aware that the ground will come out dark.

Haze is the biggest problem in cityscape photography. It is so bad at times in New York City that objects more than 500 feet away lose their color. A polarizing filter is the most effective means of eliminating haze. When it's really bad, just get as close as you can to your subject.

Architectural Details

A city's style of architecture reflects its character, be it the glass and steel newness of Houston, or the beehive of colors in downtown Tokyo. Without question, the wide-angle lens is the best tool for photographing city architecture. Very often a normal lens won't fit a large building in the image area, unless you back up across a street or plaza. Use a 24-mm, 28-mm or 36-mm lens, as well, for back-alley scenes.

When the lens is pointed upward to shoot a tall building, the vertical sides appear to tilt toward the middle of the picture.

Use creative framing to highlight architecture. Look for archways, bridge spans, and rows of support columns. Shoot through old rippled windows, lace curtains, fancy grill work, flower beds, etc.

Reflections in windows, puddles, chromed automobile ornaments, and brass door fixtures are a creative way to picture a city's images. Use a 50-mm or wide-angle lens, stopped down as far as it can go (f/16 or f/22) for lots of depth of field. Using the depth-of-field scale on the lens barrel, set the focus so that the reflecting object and the reflection are both in focus.

Mikkel Aaland: Practical and Poetic Aspects of Travel Photography

Mikkel Aaland, a San Francisco-based freelance photographer and writer, is the author of *Sweat*, a worldwide survey of saunas and sweat baths that he wrote and photographed, and *County Fair*, a collection of portraits. He also contributes to national travel and photography magazines. He approaches his work on the one hand as a practical businessman, but on the other as an artist with a commitment to the creative, almost poetic vision.

Speaking practically: "Pictures are a great way to sell stories. I can't overemphasize this, because editors are always in need of pictures to illustrate stories. If there's an eight-by-ten black-and-white glossy ready to go with your story, that may be the deciding factor convincing an editor to use your stuff—that is, if they're both decent.

"Don't go anywhere without your camera. There are certain basics you should always shoot: *An overview*, which usually tends to be taken literally from a high place. *A group shot* of several people close together. *Individual faces*, caught in good natural light. *Facades of buildings*, also shot in good natural light. *Details*, close-ups of wood carvings, rock formations, buttons."

Speaking artistically: "Step outside your rational mind when you shoot. Just react. Writers are too linear, too literal. For example, shooting signs for their words would be too literal. Shooting for their shape would be visual. Photographers should be nonlinear. Don't think. React to visual imagery. React to light. Travel photography should evoke a feeling. Be expressive. Stay loose and keep shooting. Shoot a lot; film is cheap compared to the cost of your trip. Leave room for the unexpected. Be in the moment. Photography is immediate. You can write later, but if you miss a picture, it's lost for good."

Here are some of Mikkel's road tips:

Use an x-ray bag for shipping film by air. Split up your film in three batches and mail or ship separately. Also have the film processed in separate batches. Anticipate using an average of about fifteen rolls (thirty six frames each) of film a week. But also bring more than that.

My favorite lenses: a 35-mm, a 50-mm macro, and either an 85-mm telephoto or 85-200-mm zoom lens. (For wildlife photography, bring a 300-mm telephoto lens.)

Filters: Use polarizing filters to saturate color film, but know how to use them. They work best in morning or evening when light hits the subject at indirect angles. Also use a UV (ultraviolet) filter primarily to protect the camera lens as well as cut haze.

Film: For color use Kodachrome 64 (or 25, a slower film.) Fujichrome 50 and 100 are also good, but since it is a relatively new color film its long-term stability is unproven. For black and white, Kodak's Tri-X is the standard of newspaper photographers. Ilford HP5 is also good. Both should be shot at the recommended ASA of 400. For finer grain shoot at ASA 200 with compensation in the developing.

Consider bringing two cameras, just in case one breaks.

Carry a model release form, either like the official American Society of Magazine Photographers release (see Appendix B) or a short simple version ("I hereby give you permission to use a photograph of me to accompany a newspaper or magazine article"), and ask subjects to sign it if you think there is any reason they would object to having a picture of themselves published in an editorial context. There are many gray areas to this and even professional photographers don't agree on when a model release is necessary. On this they do agree: If you plan to sell a picture that may be used in an advertisement or as a cover, then you must have a release signed. If you plan to use the photograph for editorial purposes only, it is not necessary. But to be safe, when in doubt, get a signature.

On camera bags: Opt for the utilitarian plain bag, with good shoulder straps. Fancy cases advertise your expensive equipment.

On writing and photographing simultaneously: Photograph people *after* you've interviewed people. The best portraits come when you've gotten to know somebody better. As you photograph them, keep talking to them to help them feel comfortable.

On submitting photographs to publications: Always send duplicates on speculation, never originals. (When they buy it, then send the original.) Submit sixty to one hundred color slides with a magazine story, less for newspapers. Submit ten to twelve black-and-white prints.

Buy a rubber stamp with your name, address, and phone, plus a copyright logo, and identify every slide and print you submit. For example: "Photo by MIKKEL AALAND. (C) 1988. All rights reserved. Reprint information: 415-XXX-XXXX."

Cary Wolinsky: A Photographer with a Writer's Mind

When I started freelancing, it was my good fortune to have the opportunity to work with Cary Wolinsky, a Boston-based freelance photographer who later went on to become a fulltime contract photographer for *National Geographic* magazine. More than most photographers, Cary thinks with the editorial mind of a writer. He researches his subjects extensively like any good journalist, tracking down leads, looking for angles, and following stories. Here are his tips and comments on a variety of subjects.

Researching a Trip

"Before going on a trip, travel photographers, like writers, should go to the library. Read encyclopedias and books for historical background, and magazines for more recent information. When you arrive, go to a good local bookstore and browse through relevant books. Local bookstores might have more material about the place you're in than anywhere else in the world. Also get the Yellow Pages. The phone book has leads on interesting businesses, restaurants, and gives you a sense of proportion about the place. In addition to steering you toward better picture opportunities, the knowledge you gain from the research can help you get along with local people. If you know a little about their history, who their George Washington is, they'll respond to you better."

Sending Film Home

"The safest way to get your exposed film home is to carry it back yourself. But if you need to send batches of film back, be careful: Use air freight through an international courier service. Your time and effort in getting all those may well be worth a first-class ticket home for them. In certain Third World countries, using the postal service is risky. There is some likelihood that the stamps on your package (and the package itself) will be stolen by a postal worker. Five dollars in stamps may be someone's salary for a week. If you absolutely must use the mails, bring your package to the post office and have the stamps cancelled in front of you."

Surviving the Airport

"One of the great neglected photo subjects is the airport where travelers spend so much time. The fact that modern airports are designed to make travelers as uncomfortable as possible makes for humorous pictures. Men in business suits are curled up asleep on coffee tables. Rows of people are glued to pay TVs attached to their seats. Airports are terribly emotional places. Go to any arrival gate and you'll see kissing, weeping, and hugging. You'll see anger at ticket counters and bewilderment as suitcases spill their contents onto the pavement. There's enough material at airports for a book. Bear in mind that security problems sometimes make shooting in airports more difficult."

Personal Interests

"Don't be afraid to pursue the things that interest you as a human being. Follow your curiosity. That's what makes for style in a photograph. In London, for example, they say you've just got to visit Big Ben. Though shooting Big Ben may turn out to be lucrative, personally I'm more interested in the English people and their character. So I might go to the pubs—that's where England comes alive."

Factory Tours

"More and more travelers are realizing that major industries offer free tours. Here's where you can take pictures of people in working situations. It can add a whole new aspect to your vacation to get a sense of what people really do there."

Finding Surprises

"I spent a lot of time on the road looking for surprises. The local paper is a valuable source. It not only has the weather and sunrise/sunset times, but also news and special events listings. Without a paper, you could sometimes miss a festival happening only two blocks from your hotel."

Weather

"No one except the weatherman is more aware of the weather than I am. I'm always trying to anticipate my shooting schedule based on the newspaper, airport, and TV forecasts. If you know it's going to be an unusually cool night, you can be ready to shoot mist rising off the water ten minutes after the sun hits it."

Shooting Time

"Most photographers favor early morning and evening light, and for two reasons: The colors are especially good and there is a unique peace during that first light. In predawn light, magical black shapes appear against pastel colors. Sometimes it's worthwhile to view a spot in more than one kind of light, because time of day can make it boring or spectacular."

Street Shooting

"Some photographers think the whole world is one big Disneyland. You shouldn't expect people to pose for you every time you lift up your camera. It's a privilege to photograph someone, and sometimes it must be earned. When you're after candids, put the camera up to your eye and see how people react. If they duck or hold the menu over their face, it means 'don't photograph me.' Their wish should be respected.

"Down on the docks in Charlotte Amalie, St. Thomas, in the U.S. Virgin Islands, old men sit and play dominoes. It's a really nice, colorful scene. Before I even got close, they started yelling, 'No pictures—go away!' They were tired of tourists poking lenses at them. I wanted the picture badly so I sat with them for a couple of hours. We got to know each other. Then one of the old men said, 'Why don't you take our picture? Nobody ever takes our picture. Send us some prints.' Be human, smile, and maybe you'll get the picture."

On Lenses

"Carry a wide-angle lens for candid shots. It covers more area than people realize. With a 24-mm lens, see how far away from your subject you can point the camera and still have the subject be a major part of the frame. Often this works well in a complex scene, like a marketplace, where the edges can hold the important part of the image. With careful composition, you can have relaxed and unaware subjects in your pictures, and they think you're zooming in on a banana.

"I use the fastest lens I can get because light changes so quickly from one moment to the next.

"No matter what lens you use, know how far from your subject to stand to get the right amount of coverage. I can tell now without looking through the camera. Practice and practice, like it's a musical instrument."

Photo Diplomacy

"I feel strongly about sending photo presents to everyone that I possibly can. They've done you a favor by letting you shoot them. And you don't realize how appreciated and personal your gift can be. From the practical side, if you promise a picture and don't send it, that person won't be happy about you or the next photographer coming through.

Cultural Awareness

"The first few days that you're in a new place, you notice what's unique about it. Maybe it's the native dress, or the sidewalk cafes. Little things strike you as interesting. The best time to photograph cultural details is during these first few days. After that, they tend to disappear as part of the overall scene."

Safeguarding Equipment

"If you're afraid of losing your equipment, just use some common sense. Have lockable bags, and keep them out of sight in your hotel room. Ask to not have your room cleaned, and hang up the 'Do Not Disturb' sign when you go out. Check your camera bag at the hotel desk if you won't be shooting. Be sure to have a car with a lockable trunk. Never leave your cameras out on the seat if you're leaving the car. Load and unload equipment from the trunk in places where you won't be observed."

Nuts and Bolts

- Most newspapers use black-and-white only, though more are splurging for color on the lead pages of their sections.
- When shooting with newspapers in mind, look for things that will print well, simple images, sharp contrast, close-ups of people.
- Submit five-by-seven or eight-by-ten prints, not three by fives. Unless you are a professional photographer with whom the editor is familiar, don't submit whole contact sheets. It's too much work for an editor.
- Submit mounted color slides, not unmounted color negatives, and never color prints.
- When mailing any prints, slides, or negatives, send them insured, registered, and request a return receipt so you know it got there.
- Always submit photo identifications ("captions" or "cutlines") with your images. In a simple sentence describe the scene: where, when, and what's going on. Name names when you can; editors may ask.

- If you can reproduce your black-and-white print as a high-quality photocopy, it may be cheaper if you are submitting simultaneously to many different newspapers. (That means the editors will have to call or write to you for the original—and you hope they do.) Of course, if money is no object, it's preferable to submit actual prints with articles, but when you start marketing yourself to twenty and thirty newspapers around the country, you may want to reconsider.

CHAPTER 11

Postscript from Paradise: Living Well is the Best Revenge

Here's your final exam. There is no pass or fail. There is only living life on the move, and writing as though you mean it.

WRITING ASSIGNMENT #8

POSTSCRIPT FROM PARADISE

Send me a postcard (Box 3225, Oakland, CA 94609). Send it from some wonderful destination or from your armchair, and show me—don't tell me—what it's like there today. Also, tell me if and/or how this book helped you. There's just one rule: Start with the words "Here and now I am . . ."

Bibliography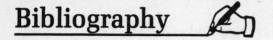

Aaland, Mikkel, *County Fair*, Santa Barbara: Capra Press, 1981.

——, *Sweat*, Santa Barbara: Capra Press, 1978.

Allen, Woody. *Side Effects*. New York: Ballantine, 1981.

Basho. *The Narrow Road to the Deep North and Other Travel Sketches*. Middlesex, England: Penguin, 1966.

Bodin, Fredrik D. *How to Get the Best Travel Photographs*. Stoneham, MA: Focal Press, 1982.

——. *The Freelance Photographer's Handbook*. Stoneham, MA: Focal Press, 1981.

Dillard, Annie. From an article in *Esquire*, March 1984.

Foster, Lee. *Lee Foster's Travel Disks*. Novato, CA: Presidio Press, 1987.

Fussell, Paul, ed. *The Norton Book of Travel*. New York: W. W. Norton, 1987.

Granta (the paperback magazine of new writing). "In Trouble Again: A Special Issue of Travel Writing." Middlesex, England: Granta Publications Ltd., Granta 20, Winter 1986.

Hemingway, Ernest. *A Farewell to Arms.* New York: Charles Scribner's Sons, 1929.

Kerouac, Jack. *Big Sur.* New York: Granada, 1980.

———. *On the Road.* New York: New American Library, 1955.

Maxey, David. "Dear Reader." *Geo,* November 1982.

Miller, Henry. *Big Sur and the Oranges of Hieronymus Bosch.* New York: New Directions, 1957.

Moore, Thomas H., ed. *Henry Miller on Writing.* New York: New Directions, 1964.

Naipaul, V. S. *Finding the Centre.* New York: Penguin, 1985.

———. *The Middle Passage.* New York: Penguin, 1978.

Neider, Charles, *The Selected Letters of Mark Twain.* New York: Harper & Row, 1982.

O'Gara, Elaine. *Travel Writer's Markets.* Berkeley, CA: Winterbourne Press, 1988.

Steinbeck, John. *Travels with Charley.* New York: Bantam, 1963.

Strunk, William Jr., and White, E. B. *The Elements of Style.* New York: Macmillan, 1972.

Theroux, Paul. *The Mosquito Coast.* New York: Avon, 1983.

Trotta, Geri. "On The Road With Marco Polo." *Travel & Leisure,* November 1983.

Twain, Mark. *The Innocents Abroad.* New York: Signet, 1966.

Tyler, Anne. *The Accidental Tourist.* New York: Berkley Books, 1986.

Winokur, Jon. *Writers on Writing.* Philadelphia: Running Press, 1986.

APPENDIX A:

Travel Writers' Resources

Travel Newsletters

Andrew Harper's Hideaway Report (Harper Associates, Inc., Box 300, Whitefish, MT 59937). Sophisticated retreats for the upper classes.

Around and About Travel (931 Shoreline Dr., San Mateo, CA 94404). For physically disabled travelers.

Consumer Reports Travel Letter (Box 53629, Boulder, CO 80322-3629). Offspring of *Consumer Reports* magazine, full of the kinds of specifics the magazine is known for.

Entree (P.O. Box 5148, Santa Barbara, CA 93150). Hot hotels and rich restaurants for the elite.

Explorer News (Foundation for Field Research, 787 South Grade Rd., Alpine, CA 92001-0380). Quarterly report on scientific expeditions for which volunteers can sign up.

Family Travel Times (80 Eighth Ave., New York, NY 10011). Family vacation tips, with day care, kids' museums etc.

First Class Confidential (824 E. Baltimore St., Baltimore, MD 21202). Black markets, secret passwords, low prices, and other collar-up travel tips.

Freighter Space Advisory (180 S. Lake Ave., Suite 335, Pasadena, CA 91101). Sail the world in cargo vessels that accommodate tourists in comfortable suites.

Gemutlichkeit (UpCountry Publishing, 3229 Round Hill Dr., Hayward, CA 94542). That's German for laid-back. Anything that fits into that category in Germany, Austria, and Switzerland.

Get Up and Go, the Mature Traveler (GEM Publishing Group, P.O. Box 50820, Reno, NV 89513). Tips for the senior set.

Grand Voyage (100 Shoreline Highway, Suite B-140, Mill Valley, CA 94941). Upscale wining, dining, and reclining.

Inside Ireland (Rookwood, Stocking Lane, Ballyboden, Dublin 16, Ireland). For the Irish-American (or Ireland-phile) who wants to return to the green paradise.

International Living (824 E. Baltimore St., Baltimore, MD 21202). Around-the-world stories in magazine style, with maps, apartment rentals, etc.

International Railway Travel (IRT, P.O. Box 35067, Louisville, KY 40232). For train travel buffs.

International Travel News (2120 28th St., Sacramento, CA 95818). Hotels, currency rates, and other reports on seventy-six countries.

Letter from London (Mary Anne Evans, 63 E. 79th St., Apt. 4-A, New York, NY 10021). Inside the city's sceniest scenes.

Links Review (Group Fore Productions, P.O. Box 10892, Chicago, IL). Profiles of golf courses around the world.

Offbeat (1250 Vallejo St., San Francisco, CA 94109). Long articles about worldwide destinations.

Specialty Travel Index (9 Mono Ave., Fairfax, CA 94930). This seventy-page booklet sells space to tour guides, outfitters, and other travel concerns, like llama trips into the Sierra Nevada, bike tours of Barbados, or boat journeys down the Nile.

Travel Europe (Box 9918, Virginia Beach, VA 23450). News on new air routes, new stores and restaurants, and much more.

Travel Fit (Box 6718, FDR Station, New York, NY 10150-1905). Fitness facilities, road races, biking tours, tennis tournaments.

Travel Smart (40 Beechdale Rd., Dobbs Ferry, NY 10522). Inside tips on hotel and airline deals, frequent-flyer programs, and unusual travel opportunities.

Unique & Exotic Travel Reporter (P.O. Box 98833, Tacoma, WA 98499, Winona M. Knutsen, editor). Visit China's Yunnan minorities. Take watercolor classes in Hawaii. Trout fish in Chile. Trek Patagonia.

Winston's Travel Deluxe (P.O. Box C, Sausalito, CA 94966). Guide to upscale resorts, inns, restaurants, with a no-nonsense ratings system.

How to Find Maps

A travel writer without a map is like a sailboat without a rudder. Most major, and even some minor, cities throughout the world now have stores that specialize in either travel accessories or maps in particular. Find a complete listing of such stores in *The Map Catalog: Every Kind of Map and Chart on Earth and Even Some Above It*, by Joel Makower, editor (New York: Vintage Books, 1986). Meanwhile here's a start for those who live near San Francisco or New York City. Call or write these places for catalogues and prices.

New York

American Map Company, 46-35 54rd Rd, Queens, NY. (can't find zip) Tel.: (718)784-0055.

Complete Traveler Bookstore, 199 Madison Ave., New York, NY 10016. Tel.: (212)679-4339.

Geographic Map Company, P.O. Box 688, Times Square Station, New York, NY 10036. Tel.: (212) 949-9100.

Traveler's Bookstore, 22 W. 52nd St., New York, NY 10019. Tel.: (212)664-0995.

The Rand McNally Map Stores: 150 E. 52nd St., New York, NY 10022. Tel.: (212)758-7488

23 E. Madison St., Chicago, IL 60602. Tel.: (312)267-6868.

595 Market St., San Francisco, CA 94105. Tel: (415)777-3131.

San Francisco

Easy Going Travel Book and Map Store, 1400 Shattuck Ave., Berkeley, CA 94709. Tel.: (415)843-3533; outside California, 1-800-233-3533).

Erickson Maps, 337 17th St., Suite 211, San Francisco, CA 94612. Tel.: (415)893-3685.

The Map Center, 2440 Bancroft Way, Berkeley, CA 94704. Tel.: (415)841-6277.

Pacific Travellers Supply, 529 State St., Santa Barbara, CA 93101. Tel.: (805)963-4438.

Phileas Fogg's Books and Maps, 87 Stanford Shopping Center, Palo Alto, CA 94304. Tel.: California, 1-800-233-3644; outside California, 1-800-533-3644.

Thomas Bros. Maps, 550 Jackson St., San Francisco, CA 94133. Tel.: (415)981-7520.

United States Geological Survey, Box 25286, Federal Center, Denver, CO 80225. Tel.: (303)236-7477.

Defense Mapping Agency. Tel.: 1-800-826-0342.

Tourism Offices for the United States and Territories

States

Alabama Bureau of Tourism and Travel
532 South Perry St., Montgomery, AL 36104-4614
Tel.: (205) 261-4169
Toll Free
In-State: 1-800-392-8096
Out-of-State: 1-800-ALABAMA
(Continental U.S.)

Alaska Division of Tourism
P.O. Box E. Juneau, AK 99811
Tel.: (907) 465-2010

Arizona Office of Tourism
1480 East Bethany Home Rd., Suite 180,
Phoenix, AZ 85014
Tel.: (602) 255-3618

Arkansas Tourism Office
One Capitol Mall, Little Rock, AR 72201
Tel.: (501) 371-1087
Toll Free
In-State: 1-800-482-8999
Out-of-State: 1-800-643-8383
(Continental U.S.)

California Office of Tourism
1121 L St., Suite 103, Sacramento, CA 95814
Tel.: (916) 322-2881
Toll Free
1-800-TO CALIF
(Continental U.S.)

Colorado Tourism Board
1625 Broadway, Suite 1700, Denver, CO 80202
Tel.: (303) 592-5410
Toll Free
1-800-433-2656
(Continental U.S.)

Connecticut Department of Economic Development
Tourism Division, 210 Washington St.,
Hartford, CT 06106
Tel.: (203) 566-3948
Toll Free
In-State: 1-800-842-7492
Out-of-State: 1-800-243-1685
(ME to VA)

Delaware Tourism Office
99 Kings Highway, Box 1401, Dover, DE 19903
Tel.: (302) 736-4271
Toll Free
In-State: 1-800-282-8667
Out-of-State: 1-800-441-8846
(Continental U.S.)

Florida Division of Tourism
126 Van Buren St., Tallahassee, FL 32301
Tel.: (904) 487-1462

Georgia Department of Industry & Trade
Tourist Division, P.O. Box 1776, Atlanta, GA 30301
Tel.: (404) 656-3590

Hawaii Visitors Bureau
P.O. Box 8527, Honolulu, HI 96815
Tel.: (808) 923-1811

Idaho Travel Council
700 W. State St., Hall of Mirrors, Second Floor, Boise, ID 83720
Tel.: (208) 334-2470
Toll Free
Out-of-State: 1-800-635-7820
(Continental U.S.)

Illinois Tourist Information Center
310 South Michigan Ave., Suite 108, Chicago, IL 60604
Tel.: (312) 793-2094
Toll Free
1-800-223-0121
(Continental U.S.)

Indiana Department of Commerce
Tourism Development Division
One North Capitol, Suite 700
Indianapolis, IN 46204
Tel.: (317) 232-8860
Toll Free
1-800-2-WANDER
(Continental U.S.)

Iowa Department of Economic Development Tourism/Film Office
200 East Grand, P.O. Box 6127, Des Moines, IA 50309
Tel.: (515) 281-3401
Toll Free
1-800-345-IOWA
(Continental U.S.)

Kansas Travel and Tourism Division
400 West 8th, 5th floor, Topeka, KS 66603
Tel.: (913) 296-2009

Kentucky Department of Travel Development
2200 Capitol Plaza Tower, Frankfort, KY 40601
Tel.: (502) 564-4930
Toll Free
1-800-225-TRIP
(U.S. & Parts of Canada)

Louisiana Office of Tourism
Attn: Inquiry Department, P.O. Box 94291, Baton Rouge, LA
70804-9291
Tel.: (504) 925-3860
Toll Free
Out-of-State: 1-800-334-8626
(Continental U.S.)

Maine Division of Tourism
Maine Publicity Bureau
97 Winthrop St., Hollwell, ME 04347-2300
Tel.: (207) 289-2423
Toll Free
1-800-533-9595
(Sept.–April: East Coast U.S.)

Maryland Office of Tourist Development
45 Calvert St., Annapolis, MD 21401
Tel.: (301) 974-3519
Toll Free
1-800-331-1750, operator 250
(Continental U.S.)

Massachusetts Division of Tourism
100 Cambridge St., 13th floor, Boston, MA 02202
Tel.: (617) 727-3201 or -3202

Toll Free
For Vacation Kit:
 1-800-942-MASS
 1-800-624-MASS
(Continental U.S.)
New England States only for summer calendar of events:
1-800-343-9072

Michigan Travel Bureau
P.O. Box 30226, Lansing, MI 48909
Tel.: (517) 373-0670
Toll Free
1-800-5432-YES
(Continental U.S.)

Minnesota Office of Tourism
375 Jackson St., 250 Skyway Level, St. Paul, MN 55101
Tel.: (612) 296-5029
Toll Free
In-State: 1-800-652-9747
Out-of-State: 1-800-328-1461
(Continental U.S.)

Mississippi Division of Tourism
P.O. Box 22825, Jackson, MS 39205
Tel.: (601) 359-3426
Toll Free
1-800-647-2290
(Continental U.S.)

Missouri Division of Tourism
P.O. Box 1055, Jefferson City, MO 65102
Tel.: (314) 751-4133

Montana Promotion Division
1424 9th Ave., Helena, MT 59620
Tel.: (406) 444-2654
Toll Free
Out-of-State: 1-800-548-3390
(Continental U.S.)

Nebraska Division of Travel and Tourism
P.O. Box 94666, Lincoln, NE 68509-4666
Tel.: (402) 471-3794
Toll Free
In-State: 1-800-742-7595
Out-of-State: 1-800-228-4307
(Continental U.S.)

Nevada Commission on Tourism
State Capitol Complex, Carson City, NV 89710
Tel.: (702) 885-3636
Toll Free
Out-of-State: 1-800-237-0774
(U.S. & Canada)

New Hampshire Office of Vacation Travel
105 Loudon Rd., P.O. Box 856, Concord, NH 03301
Tel.: (603) 271-2665
Toll Free
New England Region: 1-800-258-3608

New Jersey Division of Travel and Tourism
1 West State St., CN 826, Trenton, NJ 08625
Tel.: (609) 292-2470

New Mexico Tourism & Travel Division
Joseph M. Montoya Bldg., 1100 St. Francis St., Santa Fe, NM 87503
Tel.: (505) 827-0291

Toll Free
1-800-545-2040
(Continental U.S.)

New York State Commerce Department
One Commerce Plaza, Albany, NY 12245
Tel. (518) 474-4116
Toll Free
1-800-CALL NYS
(Continental U.S.)

North Carolina Travel and Tourism Division
430 N. Salisbury, Raleigh, NC 27611
Tel.: (919) 733-4171
Toll Free
1-800-VISIT NC
(Continental U.S.)

North Dakota Tourism Office
Liberty Memorial Bldg., Capitol Grounds,
Bismarck, ND 58505
Tel.: (701) 224-2525
Toll Free
In-State: 1-800-472-2100
Out-of-State: 1-800-437-2077
(Continental U.S.)

Ohio Division of Travel and Tourism
P.O. Box 1001, Columbus, OH 43266-0101
Tel.: (614) 466-8844
Toll Free
1-800-BUCKEYE
(Continental U.S.)

Oklahoma Tourism and Recreation Marketing Services Division
500 Will Rogers Building, Oklahoma City, OK 73105
Tel.: (405) 521-2406
Toll Free
1-800-652-6552
(Oklahoma—except OK City; AR; CO; KS; MO; NM; TX—
except area code 512)

Oregon Economic Development Department Tourism Division
595 Cottage St., N.E., Salem, OR 97310
Tel.: (503) 373-1230
Toll Free
In-State: 1-800-233-3306
Out-of-State: 1-800-547-7482
(Continental U.S.)

Pennsylvania Bureau of Travel Development
416 Forum Bldg., Dept. PR, Harrisburg, PA 17120
Tel.: (717) 787-5453
Toll Free
1-800-VISIT PA, ext. 275
(Continental U.S.)

**Rhode Island Department of Economic Development
Tourism and Promotion**
7 Jackson Walkway, Providence, RI 02903
Tel.: (401) 277-2601
Toll Free
1-800-556-2484
(ME to VA & Northern Ohio)

South Carolina Division of Tourism
1018 Ferguson St., Columbia, SC 29202
Tel.: (803) 734-0122

South Dakota Department of Tourism
Capitol Lake Plaza, 711 Wells Ave.
Pierre, SD 57501
Tel.: (605) 773-3301
Toll Free
In-State: 1-800-952-3625 or -2217
Out-of-State: 1-800-843-8000
(Continental U.S.)

Tennessee Department of Tourism Development
P.O. Box 23170, Nashville, TN 37202
Tel.: (615) 741-2158

Texas Tourist Development Agency
P.O. Box 12008, Austin, TX 78711
Tel.: (512) 462-9191

Utah Travel Council
Division of Travel Development
Council Hall/Capitol Hill, Salt Lake City, UT 84114
Tel.: (801) 533-5681

Vermont Travel Division
134 State St., Montpelier, VT 05602
Tel.: (802) 828-3236

Virginia Division of Tourism
202 North 9th St., Suite 500, Richmond, VA 23219
Tel.: (804) 786-2051
Toll Free
1-800-VISIT-VA
(Continental U.S.)

Washington State Tourism
Development Division
101 General Administration Bldg., MS AX-13, Olympia, WA
98504-0613
Tel.: (206) 753-5600
Toll Free
1-800-544-1800
(U.S.)

West Virginia Department of Commerce
Marketing/Tourism Division
2101 Washington St., E., 3rd Floor, Charleston, WV 25305
Tel.: (304) 348-2286
Toll Free
1-800-CALL WVA
(Continental U.S.)

Wisconsin Division of Tourism Development
P.O. Box 7606, Madison, WI 53707
Tel.: (608) 266-2147
Toll Free
1-800-ESCAPES
(neighboring states)

Wyoming Travel Commission
I-25 and College Dr., Cheyenne, WY 82002-0660
Tel.: (307) 777-7777
Toll Free
Out-of-State: 1-800-225-5996

District of Columbia

Washington, D.C., Convention and Visitors Association
1575 I Street, N.W., Washington, DC 20005
Tel.: (202) 789-7000

U.S. Territories

American Samoa Government
Office of Tourism
P.O. Box 1147, Pago Pago, AS 96799
Tel.: (684) 633-5187 or -5188

Guam Visitors Bureau
1200 Bay View Place, P.O. Box 1147, Pale San Vitores Rd.,
P.O. Box 3520, Agana, GU 96910
Tel.: (671) 646-5278

Marianas Visitors Bureau
P.O. Box 861, Saipan, CM, Marianas Island 96950
Tel.: (670) 234-8327

Puerto Rico Tourism Company
P.O. Box 025268, Miami, FL 33102-5268
Tel.: (212) 541-6630
Toll Free
1-800-223-6530

U.S. Virgin Islands
Division of Tourism
Box 6400, Charlotte Amalie, St. Thomas
USVI 00801
Tel.: (809) 774-8784
Toll Free
1-800-372-8784

Tourism Offices for the Caribbean Islands

Anguilla
Caribbean Tourism Association
20 East 46th St., New York, NY 10164
Tel.: (212) 682-0435

Antigua
Antigua Department of Tourism
610 Fifth Ave. New York, NY 10020
Tel.: (212) 541-4117

Aruba
Aruba Tourist Bureau
1270 Avenue of the Americas, New York, NY 10020
Tel.: (212) 246-3030

The Bahamas
Bahamas Tourist Office
150 East 52nd St., New York, NY 10022
Tel.: (212) 758-2777

Barbados
Barbados Board of Tourism
800 Second Ave., New York, NY 10017
Tel.: (212) 986-6516

British Virgin Islands
British Virgin Islands Tourist Board
370 Lexington Ave., New York, NY 10017
Tel.: (212) 696-0400

Cayman Islands
Cayman Islands Tourist Board
420 Lexington Ave., New York, NY 10170
Tel.: (212) 682-5582

Curaçao
Curaçao Tourist Board
400 Madison Ave., Suite 311, New York, NY 10017
Tel.: (212) 751-8266

Grenada
Grenada Department of Tourism
14 East 44th St., New York, NY 10017
Tel.: (212) 687-9554

Guadeloupe
French West Indies Tourist Board
610 Fifth Ave., New York, NY 10020
Tel.: (212) 757-1125

Jamaica
Jamaica Tourist Board
866 Second Ave., New York, NY 10017
Tel.: (212) 688-7650

Martinique
French West Indies Tourist Board (see above)

Puerto Rico
Commonwealth of Puerto Rico Tourism Company
1290 Avenue of the Americas, Suite 2230, New York, NY. 10104
Tel.: (212) 541-6630

St. Barthélemy
French West Indies Tourist Board (see above)

St. Lucia
St. Lucia Tourist Board
41 East 42nd St., New York, NY 10017
Tel.: (212) 867-2950

St. Martin, Dutch side
St. Maarten/Saba/St. Eustatius Tourist Information Office
275 Seventh Ave., New York, NY 10001
Tel.: (212) 989-0000
French side
French West Indies Tourist Board (see above)

Trinidad and Tobago
Trinidad and Tobago Tourist Board
400 Madison Ave., New York, NY 10017
Tel.: (212) 838-7750

U.S. Virgin Islands
U.S. Virgin Island Division of Tourism
1270 Avenue of the Americas, New York, NY 10020
Tel.: (212) 582-4520

European Travel Commission
630 Fifth Avenue, New York, NY 10111
(Phone (212) 307-1200)

Members

Dr. Walter Klement
Austrian National Tourist Office
500 Fifth Avenue
New York, NY 10110
(212) 944-6880

Mrs. Frederique Raeymaekers
Belgian Tourist Office
745 Fifth Avenue
New York, NY 10151
(212) 758-8130

Mr. Dennis Droushiotis
Cyprus Tourism Organization
13 East 40th Street
New York, NY 10016
(212) 213-9100

Mr. Tom Sodemann
Danish Tourist Board
655 Third Avenue
New York, NY 10017
(212) 949-2333

Mr. Pekka Kurki
Finnish Tourist Board
655 Third Avenue
New York, NY 10017
(212) 949-2333

Mr. Michel Bouquier
French Government Tourist Office
610 Fifth Avenue
New York, NY 10020
(212) 757-1125

Dr. John Martin
German National Tourist Office
747 Third Avenue
New York, NY 10017
(212) 308-3300

Mr. Donald L. Ford
British Tourist Authority
40 W. 57th Street
New York, NY 10019
(212) 581-4708

Mr. George Kouros
Greek National Tourist Organization
645 Fifth Avenue
New York, NY 10022
(212) 421-5777

Mrs. Unnur Kendall Georgsson
Iceland Tourist Board
655 Third Avenue
New York, NY 10017
(212) 949-2333

Mr. Niall Millar
Irish Tourist Board
757 Third Avenue
New York, NY 10017
(212) 418-0800

Mr. Umberto Lombardi
Italian Government Travel Office
630 Fifth Avenue
New York, NY 10111
(212) 245-4825

Ms. Anne Bastian
Luxembourg National Tourist Office
801 Second Avenue
New York, NY 10017
(212) 370-9850

Mr. George Vella
Consulate of Malta
249 East 35th Street
New York, NY 10016
(212) 725-2345

Ms. Maguy Maccario
Monaco Gov't Tourist & Convention Bureau
845 Third Avenue-2nd Floor
New York, NY 10022
(212) 759-5227

Mr. Stephen J. Hodes
Netherlands Board of Tourism
355 Lexington Avenue
New York, NY 10017
(212) 370-7360

Mr. Bard Andreas Schjolberg
Norwegian Tourist Board
655 Third Avenue
New York, NY 10017
(212) 949-2333

Mr. Carlos Lameiro
Portuguese National Tourist Office
548 Fifth Avenue
New York, NY 10036
(212) 354-4403

Mr. Auerlio Torrente
National Tourist Office of Spain
665 Fifth Avenue
New York, NY 10022
(212) 759-8822

Mr. Ed Conradson
Swedish Tourist Board
655 Third Avenue
New York, NY 10017
(212) 949-2333

Mr. Chris Zoebeli
Swiss National Tourist Office
608 Fifth Avenue
New York, NY 10017
(212) 757-5944

Mr. Oktay Ataman
Turkish Culture & Information Office
821 United Nations Plaza
New York, NY 10017
(212) 687-2194

Ms. Vesna Loney
Yugoslav National Tourist Office
630 Fifth Avenue
New York, NY 10111
(212) 757-2801

APPENDIX B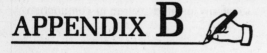

The Standard
Photo Release

I also consent to the use of any printed matter in conjunction therewith.

I hereby waive any right that I may have to inspect or approve the finished product or products or the advertising copy or printed matter that may be used in connection therewith or the use to which it may be applied.

I hereby release, discharge and agree to save harmless _____ _____, his legal representatives or assigns, and all persons acting under his permission or authority or those for whom he is acting, from any liability by virtue of any blurring, distortion, alteration, optical illusion, or use in composite form, whether intentional or otherwise, that may occur or be produced in the taking of said picture or in any subsequent processing thereof, as well as any publication thereof even though it may subject me to ridicule, scandal, reproach, scorn and indignity.

I hereby warrant that I am of full age and have every right to contract in my own name in the above regard. I state further that I have read the above authorization, release and agreement, prior to its execution, and that I am fully familiar with the contents thereof.

Dated: _____

_____
_____
_____
                        (Address)

_____
    (Witness)